Constant Cravings

One Man's True Story of His Struggle with Prescription Drug Addiction

Mike Dryden

Eloquent Books
New York, New York

Eloquent Books
An imprint of AEG Publishing Group
845 Third Avenue, 6th Floor — #6016
New York, NY 10022
www.eloquentbooks.com

ISBN: 978-1-60693-130-1
SKU: 1-60693-130-X

Printed in the United States of America

Dedication

*To Jackie and Dani, whose unconditional
love and support made this book possible.
Thanks also to the God centered 12-step
groups and the fellowship they offer.*

*"Religion is for people afraid of going to Hell.
Spirituality is for those who have already
been there."*

—Unknown

Contents

1

Here I lay next to my wife, Jackie, of 35 years. I love her so much, more than my own life, that's for sure. I have a headache tonight, not so unusual for me, also this thing going on in my stomach for the second day now. It's no surprise I can't sleep tonight with things going on, along with the fact that I just quit my job of eleven years yesterday.

None of this bothers me as much as the other feeling I'm having as I lay here; the overwhelming desire to wake up my wife and have her take me to the ER, where I know I can get something to make me feel better. This is old behavior. I've been clean and sober for some time now and around the tables of twelve step meetings for eight or nine years. But as of this moment I'm out there, in a place in my head I shouldn't be. Everything seems so out of whack. I've just left God's world and re-entered my own, a dangerous place to be. I often call it my AK-47 side. My head and my physical being crave some instant gratification. I'm hurting physically, mentally and spiritually. I don't want to feel anything right now. I'm laying here questioning God's will and purpose for my life.

I'm 53 years old and didn't graduate from high school, but did receive my G.E.D. I know finding a job that I won't soon end up hating will be extremely difficult. My top two prospects are returning to being a youth counselor or working with the handicapped, both have a high burn out rate, or they do for me anyway.

People say that I care too much and will eventually succumb to the ways of the world again. But for me that means returning to pills and alcohol because I can't be part of the material world without them. The spiritual world, God's world, is the only place that I've found true peace and hope in an often time hopeless world.

It's a strange night and morning as Daylight Savings Time started three weeks early this year. So I lay here staring at the clock. It says almost 12:30 A.M., Sunday, March 11, but we set the clocks ahead one hour before going to bed so it's really 11:30 P.M., Saturday night, March 10th. That's not the only change though; the weather has changed drastically, from a very cold and snowy February and March. On March 1st and 2nd we had a blizzard in our area and 20 inches of snow. Now the weather is sunny and warm.

Normally with no job to go to I would be here in bed daydreaming about my first fishing trip after a long winter, but as nice as it is, even a forecast for the mid 70's by Tuesday, there is still ice cover on the lakes here in west central Iowa. You see, fishing is my only real escape when I'm actively keeping clean and sober. It's God's gift to me. Pills and alcohol were my gift to me and ultimately robbed me of going fishing.

A few hours earlier my wife and I, along with our youngest daughter, Dani, returned from Des Moines. We attended an Amnesty International meeting in support of Ruth Ann, a young girl who is serving a life sentence without parole at the Mitch-ellville Institute for Women. Ruth Ann was charged with murder at the age of 14 and will soon turn 29 years old in prison. The three of us set up a display with information and pictures of Ruth Ann. I read a letter to those in attendance that Ruth Ann wrote for this event.

So as I lay here in bed rehashing these current events and changes, focusing on my migraine and stomach pain, I turn toward Jackie who is sound asleep.

"Hon, wake up," I said as I shook her lightly, "I need to go to the hospital."

"What's wrong? Do you have a migraine?" she asked.

"Yes," I answered, "but this stomach pain is unbearable."

That was a mild exaggeration. So as she has done so many times in the past, Jackie got out of bed, got dressed and took me to the ER. I knew what I wanted and convinced myself due to the stress of these current events that I needed it. First I endured an injection of Toradol, a mild pain reliever, which I knew I would have to go through to get the good stuff. Three injections of Morphine later I was starting to feel better, or, should I say, not feeling all that emotional pain, and of course, those physical pains had vanished as well. They would send me home with six tablets of Vicodin that I would take in one dose because that's what I do and a prescription for twenty more, insuring that I would have at least one more day of comfort. When looking back, now a few days later, I think of the doctor and nurses who provided me with such care and compassion as they performed their duties and tried to ease my pain. I think of the young man who was there with his ailing grandma in real pain and how I was robbing them of the 100 percent of medical attention she should be receiving. I think of the x-ray technician that was on call who had to be awakened at home to come in and take my stomach x-ray. I realized more than ever that I didn't want to return to this lifestyle of using people instead of caring for them and helping them.

How did all this begin? How did a man of such faith become an alcoholic and prescription drug addict? Let's start at the beginning and work our way back to the present.

2

I was born September 17, 1953, the child of an alcoholic father. My dad worked hard but drank harder. Some time after dad passed, one of his friends told me, "Mike, nobody drank like your dad." My dad was a good man, but alcohol is an equal opportunity destroyer, it can make a good person do bad things. I know it can make us say things to our children and loved ones that they carry with them the rest of their lives.

I remember when I was about five years old, my dad put me on his knee and asked me what I thought of him leaving and living somewhere else. Things weren't going well at home with his marriage of many years to my mom. It was his drinking that caused most of the problems and, of course, his problem became our problem.

This is the nature of the disease; that trickle down effect that ultimately creates a dysfunctional family. I have forgiven him and often times wish he were still around today so I could talk to him about my recovery from alcohol and drugs. There were so many events growing up that I pledged I would never put my kids through. Baseball games without dad being there or showing up under the influence of alcohol. Fishing trips never came around or were dampened by drinking, criticism and anger. Oh yes, dad had an anger problem, as do I. It wasn't always a good idea to have friends over to the house unless dad was at work.

Dad was in a severe one car accident when I was a pre-teen, where, except for the grace of God he would have died. He left a bar in our hometown very late and very intoxicated. It was told he could barely walk, let alone drive. Back in those days drunk driving was almost normal, not the terrible thing it is today.

The good ol' boys in the bar just let him go, knowing he would be driving some 25 miles to another town. Finally, one of them decided to go follow him. He caught up to my dad only after the accident had occurred. As the story goes dad had missed a sharp curve in the road and went airborne, just missing a car on the gravel road at the stop sign. A 14-year-old driver with his learner's permit and his mother occupied that car. I've been told that the young driver backed up and got out of my dad's way. When dad's friend arrived an ambulance was already there. My dad was stumbling around in shock with one ear dangling by a piece of skin.

His car, a 1962 Ford Galaxy was crushed like a pancake. The irony is that possibly only his severe drunkenness saved his life as he was tossed around like a rag doll. His friend meantime is arguing with the ambulance driver that he should take dad with him. The driver replied, "The only place your friend is going is to the hospital and probably for a long time." Dad was in critical condition and was hospitalized for a lengthy period of time.

I also remember as a child hearing things like, 'Dad's drinking binge lasted for days in an out of town hotel,' and then being found under a bridge and words I didn't understand like, 'He was having DT's,' and thought he was covered with spiders. One of his friends once told me that after dad returned home from a long stay in an alcohol treatment center that his first words were 'my liver's okay,' meaning he could drink some more.

Mom worked hard at menial, low-paying jobs to cover the money that dad foolishly spent. Our family was gradually torn apart, each member assuming their role in the stereotypical alcoholic family. My older brother and sister took the brunt of the abuse along with my mother. My younger brother, who was just an infant during the worst of times, seemed to escape without much emotional wreckage. I guess I would describe myself as the 'lost child.' I remember my older brother enlisting in the Marines during the Vietnam War. I can't help but believe that dad played an instrumental role in his wanting to get out of the house and prove maybe to dad that he was a man.

Dad was very hard on Ted during events like getting his first car, a whopping 50 dollars and at his baseball games being very vocal and critical and in drunken outbursts telling him that he would never amount to anything. So off to Vietnam he went, a place called Da-Nang, to the front lines for close to six months. This was very stressful on mom and us kids at home. I remember gathering around the TV set for the six o'clock news each evening where they would talk about the war; things like enemy casualties versus American G.I. body bag counts. I know this took an enormous toll on my mother and us.

Ted was discharged from the Marines after receiving shrapnel wounds in combat. He had tough life experiences since returning home to say the least. He had two or three marriages ending in divorce and a nearly 30-year-old son living in the same state that he rarely or never sees. He's pretty much a loner and isolates with fishing and hunting, possibly his only true loves. We live just miles apart and hardly ever see each other unless it's by chance when we're at the same lake fishing. Then, of course, the family curse of alcohol and drugs has been his constant companion along with the loving dog sitting beside him for the comfort that seems to elude him. I love you Ted, I always have. I just wanted to let you know that.

My mom and dad finally divorced when I was approximately twelve or thirteen. This is when my rebellion years began. I started on a series of random acts of violence. Vandalism topped the list. If there were a window and a rock nearby the glass would soon shatter. Breaking and entering also became exciting and no car, house, business or even a church, in one sad case, were off limits. This emotional baggage of guilt, shame and remorse is still carried with me today.

Later in adulthood, there weren't enough painkillers available to quiet the voices of some of those events of my teenage years. Binge drinking became frequent back then. My friends and I would drink any alcohol we could get our hands on. We would do almost anything on a dare. Fast cars and being on the police's 'Most Watched List' was so exciting. I once stole my own mother's treasured old coin collection for gas money to run away. Cutting myself with razor blades or other sharp objects seemed to give me some kind of twisted high also. The criminal adventure I was on ended in four jail sentences and eventually a seven-month stay in the Quakerdale Home for Boys in New Providence, Iowa.

3

At age seventeen my life changed suddenly and dramatically. On the streets of my hometown there appeared a 1965 blue Ford Mustang, proudly bearing California license plates. The car held a distant second to the most beautiful, blonde haired girl this troubled boy had ever laid eyes on. I believe in rare cases love at first sight actually happens. God placed Jackie in my life and his timing is always perfect. Driving the drag is what young people did back then and every time her Mustang would meet my 61 Chevy we would give each other the peace sign. How romantic was that? I had to meet this girl, but I knew half the guys in town had the same idea. Jackie's dad was soon to retire as captain of the San Diego Fire Department so she and her mom were in town looking for an apartment.

Jackie's mom was from nearby Templeton so they decided to relocate here. I finally found the courage to speak to her and one year later we were married. We were both eighteen years old. Our first car, purchased by her dad, was a red 1963 Chevy SS. Wow! It didn't get any better than that. My mother and father-in-law moved out of their small apartment so we could move in. All was blissful, but minor details like me getting a real job and growing up still lay ahead. That next year Jackie gave birth to our first daughter, Janna.

That first real job came at Casey's General Store here in Carroll where I held the position of assistant manager. Casey's, a fast growing convenience store chain soon promoted me to manager at their new store in Pocahontas, some fifty miles away.

So as Jackie nurtured our infant daughter, I drove to and from my new job, sometimes twice a day. We soon moved to Pocahontas and purchased our first home, a modest trailer settled in a mobile home park. Pocahontas, a town with a population of about 2,000, was small town living at its finest. I joined a young men's club called the Jaycees, and through many hours behind the counter at Casey's we made many friends.

Simple things like bowling, fishing and playing cards at each other's homes seemed good and right. Back then I rarely drank and enjoyed soft drinks while bowling instead of beer as many did, and as far as pills, maybe an occasional aspirin for a headache, but that was it. Things weren't always that rosy for a twenty-year-old store manager though. Power struggles with employees often ended with me doing menial tasks that I wanted done around the store. One of my many character defects, perfectionism, soon reared its ugly head. I not only stocked the walk-in cooler, but found myself turning pop and beer cans so the label was in front.

Upper management would often bring franchise prospects to my store because of its appearance. This self-induced stress, even at such a young age, brought about a two-week nosebleed that ended up with me in a nearby hospital. This turned out to be the first in a lifelong series of times that God spared my life, as loosing so much blood became quite serious.

In March of 1976 our second daughter, Sasha, was born in Pocahontas. After a couple of years of being a store manager and the stress associated with it, I became restless and started looking at other job possibilities. In nearby Spencer they were looking for a beer truck salesman at a new Coors distributorship. Spencer, a much larger town, seemed to offer more possibilities. I applied for and got the job as a route salesman for Coors, selling and delivering beer to our accounts. We had our mobile home moved to a trailer park in Spencer. Jackie and I knew we would miss our friends in Poky, appropriately called the Princess City. Our girls, barely five and two, just wanted to go with mom and dad, wherever that may be.

My father, Jack, back in Carroll, must have been concerned. He had been a truck driver for thirty-three years and knew the hardships. Also being a struggling alcoholic, in his own white knuckling will-power attempts to stay sober, may also have had some concern that I was now in the beer business, and he had a good reason to. The beer was mostly free for me to drink and I had always loved Coors. To top it off, Coors was refrigerated in our warehouse and kept cold in our trucks. After a long days work several ice cold beers tasted mighty good and the price was right. Oh yes, an occasional one off the truck during working hours, along with one or two at the many bars I delivered to.

Can you imagine the insanity of driving a beer truck that not only is loaded, but so is the driver? I worked hard for the money and unknowingly; I drank to numb my feelings. We did many Coors nights at area bars to promote our product, which meant more free beer and companionship. Most everyone, it seemed, loved a beer man, but as time went by I started not loving me so much. My employment at Coors lasted nearly ten years. Our daughters Janna and Sasha were now 15 and 12.

Toward the end of my ten years with Coors Janna revealed to us that she was pregnant at the age of 15 and only a sophomore in high school. We soon learned that Janna had been having alcohol and drug problems of her own. This eventually led to treatment and a short-term group home.

4

On May 27, 1989, Danielle arrived. She was our first grandchild. I was a grandpa at the age of thirty-five. Dani was born with Type B Strep, a form of pneumonia that affects newborns, and we almost lost her after only seeing her for a few precious minutes. Our doctor in Spencer, Dr. D, is credited for saving Dani's life. Our pastor came to the hospital and baptized her with an eyedropper of water and God's word of hope. Dani was then flown to Sioux Falls, South Dakota still in critical condition. Jackie and I didn't have a clue back then what God had in store for us with this miracle child.

That next day, after giving birth, Janna, barely sixteen, and I drove the two hours from Spencer to Sioux Falls. It was touch and go for Baby Dani for many days, but after two weeks she finally returned home with us. She was still hooked up to a portable sleep apnea machine that measured her heart rate and respirations. We set Janna up in a modest apartment equipped with the initial needs for a new mom and infant. Janna not only was sixteen, but like her father she was a bit of a rebel, and soon returned to her past behavior. Dani was only weeks old when

Jackie and I brought her home with us. Janna stayed in the apartment. With Janna's behavior and lack of parenting skills we all agreed that Jackie and I would acquire custody and guardianship of Dani. At the age of seven, with Dani and Janna's approval, she was adopted by us. Our first grandchild was now our seven-year-old daughter, God's miracle still being fulfilled.

When Dani was just one I got a steady job again. After abruptly quitting the beer business back when first learning Janna was pregnant, I didn't work much at all. This was a painful time for me as I deeply regretted leaving my job at Coors, but God had other plans for my life, and I truly believe this plan was for me to go to work at Forest Ridge Community Youth Services not far from Spencer. To the town of Estherville, I would be a youth counselor, a far cry from my previous job. I liked the idea of helping kids and I had been in a home such as this back when I was 15 years old.

I would spend the early 1990's at Forest Ridge driving back and forth from Spencer. Most of my shifts were four days on, four days off, with Jackie at home raising Danielle, just a toddler by then. I worked at the 30-day shelter and then at the different long-term boys and girls cottages. The kids were mostly in the 12 through 17-year range and a six to 12 month stay was the norm. Since I couldn't fix my own teenager at home, maybe, just maybe, I could help these troubled teens; and it went pretty well at first. Then, dealing with uncooperative parents combined with some kids that just didn't seem to get it, I started to feel the stress. These kids suffered much abuse so early in life and I listened and tried to help during our group sessions, and then the migraine headaches started. I had terrible fire-like pain in my temples that lasted for days at a time. I was constantly on the defense, fearing my next migraine.

I also suffered through the loss of two special kids that I had counseled and became close to. Kent was a young man at the age of fifteen, full of life, energy and dreams. His room was located next to our staff bedroom. I especially recall a broken arm he received playing some activity around the cottage during his last days. Each night before his shower he would knock on the staff door and smile. "Mr. D., would you wrap my cast so I can take a shower?"

I would proceed to put a bread bag or other plastic wrap over his cast fastened with rubber bands. Kent had one of those infectious smiles that probably would have opened a lot of doors for him if he would have had the chance to pursue his dreams. Christmas soon came and I took Kent to his home in a near by city along with some other residents to spend the holidays with their families. Home visits like these weren't uncommon. When it came time to pick Kent and the others up, the weather took a turn for the worse. High winds blowing around the snow that was already on the ground created blizzard type conditions.

We as staff, and I as the driver, decided to wait one extra day before making the two-hour trip. So the kids had another day reprieve on their home visits. It turned out to be a deadly day though for Kent. That night, or so it goes, he went to meet some friends. Someone there had access to a handgun and it was passed around, each boy examining it and handing the loaded gun to the next in line. When it was given to Kent it went off, striking him first in the arm and then passing through his head. Kent died instantly.

I'll never forget picking the other kids up the next day. I had to make up some story as to why we wouldn't be picking up Kent. I tried to keep the radio off, fearing there would be a news report on his death. Staff had decided before I left just to get the other kids back to the cottage where we could tell them properly. A minister was brought in with the extra counselors. We called all the boys together and proceeded to tell them what happened. This was extremely hard on me as I tried to console Kent's friends and roommates. Who would console the counselors? We were hurting too, each in our own way. The phone rang during group; it was my wife back in Spencer. All it took was the sound of her voice and I started crying uncontrollably.

The funeral was also extremely hard as staff transported some of Kent's friends who wanted to attend. One of his favorite songs was "Something to Believe In." Many tears flowed as we all searched our hearts for something to believe in. Why did this happen? What if... ? What if I had only braved the weather and picked Kent up on time? What if... ?

Ruth Ann, a beautiful fourteen year old, six foot tall girl, would be another painful loss for me. I was her counselor also for a few short months while I worked at one of the girls cottages. I attended her basketball and volleyball games, two sports she loved and excelled at. The time soon came for Ruth Ann to return home, something I hated seeing many of these kids have to do.

My wife, Jackie, and I along with two-year-old Dani, took Ruth Ann out for pizza the night before she would be discharged. A short time later, Ruth Ann, on the run and desperate, was charged with murder. Still only fourteen years old she was tried as an adult and basically received her own death sentence; life in prison without the possibility of parole. Thrown in with adult inmates at such a young age has taken a toll on her. The same questions came to mind as the night Kent died. Why? What if... ? Could I possibly have done something to prevent this?

5

I left my job as a youth counselor after only three years. I was emotionally burned out and those terrible headaches wouldn't go away. I sought pain treatment through chiropractors, doctors, bio-feed back, neurologists, home remedies and relaxation tapes. By this time I was eating Excedrin, up to ten a day. There was a chronic pain clinic in town and I was soon sent there. They searched for pressure points on my nerve endings and other things like that. After unsuccessful attempts to ease my headache pain I was given some information that would drastically change my life over the next twelve or more years. I was thirty-eight years old at that time. The physician informed me of a new medication about to hit the pharmacy shelves. She said the new medicine was a narcotic nose-spray called Stadol. I remember that at the time the word 'narcotic' didn't really mean much to me. I pretty much thought it was the word for street drugs. I would soon fall in love with this word.

Up to this point it had been O.T.C painkillers such as Excedrin or Advil. So off to my family doctor I went and asked about this new nose-spray. He told me the medical profession had been anxiously awaiting the arrival of Stadol. They thought because it was a nose-spray and not a pill that its addictive potential would be much lower. One spray, one nostril is how it was prescribed. That was all it took and, wow! Not only did the headache go away, but so did leg aches, backaches and other minor physical pains. The real miracle, so it seemed, was that my emotional pain was numbed also. I felt great! Alcohol brought on a numbness of its own, but not like this! Being tired, sleepy or drained during the day was never enjoyable, but this was different. The slow fading in and out of consciousness was awesome. The next four years, while Jackie worked, often six days a week, I stayed home. Headaches were my excuse and I still had my share of them, but just sitting around the house drugged-up became my favorite pastime. Because, as I believe, "Once your snake-bitten by the drug dragon you crave the venom for the rest of your life."

I missed a lot during that four-year absence from reality. Dani suddenly went from three to seven. I, meanwhile, had thought I had discovered the answer to all of my problems. I started looking forward to headaches. At first everything seemed better, but my pleasant world soon turned insane. The prescribed dose for Stadol was one spray in one nostril. I soon discovered that a spray in both nostrils increased the effect. One bottle was intended to last one month. It soon became my own prescribed dosage when I felt the need not the feel. A vial of Stadol soon would last me only two or three days. I often sought out prescriptions with 12 refills, intended to last for year. In a couple months I was soon seeking more. The pharmacies were concerned, but I quickly learned the right strings to pull to get what I wanted. After all, I didn't just want the effects of this drug, I needed them. Even if it meant being dishonest to everyone, including my family.

I did land a $6.00 an hour job as a security guard at a local industry. The Stadol was always my constant companion. It could always be found in my desk drawer. I was required to make hourly rounds often times filling my nose before or after making a round. The majority of the time I just sat at the desk staring out the window with the radio on as I mellowed out in that semi-conscious state of mind I had grown to love. The insanities that go hand in hand with drug abuse started show-ing up. Jackie was starting to get concerned with my self-cen-tered life. When my supply had run out I would do whatever it took to get my next high. This habit was expensive and it took its toll on our modest incomes. One Sunday afternoon as I sat at my work desk and out of Stadol, I called Jackie who was vis-iting one of our daughters. I used my best 'poor-me-in-pain' voice as I persuaded her to go to a pharmacy and spend the $70 we didn't have to get me that brown vial of relief. I knew by the sound of her voice that Jackie was disgusted and angry so the wheels in my head started to spin to come up with a way to prove to her I was really sick. I poured water on my blue work shirt and smeared it around so I could tell her I had been vomiting.

As time went by I proceeded to go downhill. Old childhood behaviors started to return. Stealing, lying, cutting myself and immoral thoughts and desires. I used anything and anyone to get my drug. Jackie's dad, with his big heart, would often go and get me a refill, pay for it and deliver it to me at work. I even left my post a couple of times using the company car to run to the pharmacy on weekends. I interfered in the lives of so many people who didn't want to see me in pain. One fourth of July found me at work craving my Stadol and being a holiday, the pharmacy was closed. After my pleading to Jackie about how much pain I was in she called the pharmacist at his home some 25 miles away. Because of his caring attitude toward his customers he drove into town, opened the pharmacy and got me a refill. Our local church even gave us emergency fund money so we could get groceries because we were spending so much on doctor bills and painkillers.

6

Finally, our family doctor, backed into a corner with the addiction I kept denying, made a decision. I would be sent to a Sioux Falls, South Dakota hospital to first be weaned off the Stadol, and then they would evaluate my headaches. This process would take one week and I promised to be motivated and sincere in an effort to find a non-narcotic relief for my headaches. I must admit now though, that the dangling carrot that got me there was the fact that they would give me doses of Stadol and slowly taper me off. In my heart I truly wanted help. I didn't like the person I had become. I had little or no drive, let alone hopes and dreams, and this anger problem was now on steroids, so to say. Uncontrollable outbursts weren't uncommon. Once even, to a highway patrolman who's only fault was that he pulled me over for not wearing a seatbelt.

After about the third day of treatment I was given what was to be my last dose of Stadol. I panicked later that night and with total disregard for the reason I was there, and my family with all their trust back home, I reacted insanely to the first stages of this disease called drug addiction. My room was located just off the nurse's station and I knew what drawer my Stadol was in. Normally it was locked up immediately after they gave it to me. It was late at night and there was only one visible nurse who had left the keys in the medicine drawer as she ran off to help a patient in need. I was hooked up to an I.V. on a large, movable stand that was dispensing a harmless fluid into my vein, but even this obstacle was not going to stop my next move. I crawled out of bed and proceeded to roll the stand out to the nurse's station. I could hear the nurse in another room talking to a patient. I pulled on the drawer and as it opened I saw the container of Stadol. I backed up into my room and dispensed the rest of the bottle up my nose. Totally ignoring the consequences of my actions, I placed the bottle back in the drawer and returned to bed. I may have gotten away with this self-will run riot, but I paid the price a few hours later.

Despite all the painkillers in my system I got one of the worst migraines ever. I was told there was nothing staff could do until my doctor arrived in the morning. I was on a "no narcotic" order and would have to wait for the doctor to administer an I.V of a non-narcotic DHE, a very effective medicine for migraine pain. So there I sat, on the edge of my bed in extreme pain, holding the hand of the compassionate nurse who came in to comfort me. Poetic justice, I thought, as I sat there in my own shit. I caused this mess and didn't think I would soon forget this painful lesson, but I did. True insanity is doing the same thing over and over, expecting different results. Unbeknownst to me, a lot of painful lessons lay ahead.

Jackie brought me home after my week was up. She was hopeful that this headache, narcotic thing was behind us. I quickly shattered that dream the very day we returned home. That night I persuaded her to take me to the ER where I could receive a shot of Demerol. Jackie's love for me was, and is, so strong, so unconditional, that she seldom questioned the pain I claimed to be in.

Toward the end of my four-year love affair with Stadol, my dad became very ill back in our hometown. We decided to put our house up for sale and move back to Carroll. Jackie was all for this idea, as Spencer wasn't her favorite place, but Carroll, the town where we first met, oh yes, she loved Carroll. So, maybe she thought I would return to that drug-free happy man she married so long ago. We soon sold the house and moved back to our hometown. Our daughter changed schools, leaving behind friends, Sasha was now on her own and Janna was married. As for me, I loved Spencer, there were lakes to fish around every corner and I fished them all. I had a lot of fear about returning to the town I grew up in but hoped this move would fix me. But guess what? When we settled in Carroll I looked in the mirror and I saw the same prescription drug addict that lived in Spencer. We made several thousand dollars in profit when we sold our house and I proceeded to spend a great deal of it on Stadol.

My dad soon passed away. We were all there in the hospital room, I was going to the restroom frequently to pump some more of that crap up my nose. I was holding Dad's hand when he took his last breath. Was I going to break this family cycle of addiction or pass it on to my kids? I loved my dad. He did the best he could with the demons that accompany alcoholism.

7

I started my first real job in Carroll, since my days as a youth counselor, at a large, local distributing company. I had been there only a few days when I had my last and perhaps one of my most insane Stadol incidents. I was in between refills, a dangerous place for me to be as this was when the most anger, anxiety and panic set in. I found myself a place to hide at my new job, pulled a box cutter out of my pocket and took a serious swipe at my left arm. I inflicted a very deep, six inch gash and real pain set in. I removed my shirt and wrapped it around my sliced arm. I went outside, climbed into a company vehicle and drove myself to the ER. No one at work knew anything until I called from the hospital to report my accident. Yes, I reported it as an accident. What else could I say it was? The truth wasn't an option at the time. So I walked into the ER bleeding profusely. I told them about my so-called 'accident' and they proceeded to sew me up with several stitches, including four to close up the artery I severed. I managed to con the doctor out of three bottles of Stadol for pain relief and in a sick way it all seemed worth it. I remained employed at the company for 11 years, always carrying my guilt, shame and remorse around silently.

I tried making amends by being a good employee, doing extra little things and helping out by staying late, but addiction is cunning, baffling and powerful and it was in my life to stay and wreak even more havoc. I soon graduated to pills, narcotic painkillers and tranquilizers. I thought I had discovered yet another utopia. The effects of some of these pills were better and longer lasting than my favorite nose spray. After all, I told myself, this Stadol was driving me crazy. What else could have caused so much insanity in my life and in my behavior? I thought back to the time when, in a state of withdrawal, I conjured up this idea of how I could get another Stadol refill after just emptying one in two days. "I had to have it," wasn't just an excuse anymore. I put water in an empty brown Stadol bottle to just the right level. My intent was to plug the sprayer so I could return it to the pharmacy and tell them it was defective. So off I went, and it was much too easy. I put a toothpick in the sprayer and broke it off and sure enough, it wouldn't spray. It only oozed out water, not medicine. He handed me a new bottle and off I went.

In my state of mind at the time I tried to justify my actions. I was living in a constant state of fear and hopelessness. I don't blame the Stadol or the drug company that makes it anymore than an alcoholic can blame Anheuser-Busch for making Budweiser. I don't blame the doctors, nurses or pharmacists, just as an alcoholic can't blame the club owner for dispensing alcohol. I actively sought it out and wouldn't take no for an answer. The final blow against Stadol came when I watched a newscast called *Nightline* hosted by Ted Koppel. The show that night was on Stadol and the negative side to this painkiller you sprayed up your nose. They reported 53 deaths to date associated with the drug. Stadol was now called 'very addictive with a high abuse potential.' Violent behavior from previously non-violent people was linked to the use of this drug, combined with alcohol and other drugs. So I parted company with my friend in a spray bottle and entered the pill playground.

8

Xanax, a tranquilizer, and Darvocet, a mild narcotic pain reliever, were my first experience with mood altering pills. After spending many hours on the computer at medical websites and turning the pages of the recent P.D.R (Physicians Desk Reference) I sought out pills that would numb my feelings the most. I used any physical ailment imaginable along with my anxiety, depression and sleep disorder to get my pills. The list of narcotic painkillers, tranquilizers and sedatives I would try over the next few years grew in length. Fiorinal, Fioricet, Tylenol #3, Tylenol #4, all with codeine. Darvocet with propoxyphene. Vicodin, Vicoprofen, Lortab, with hydrocodone. Tylox, Percodan, Percocet with oxycodone. Demerol, Morphine, Nubain, Dilaudid and Methadone. Ultram and Ultracet with Tramadol. Valium, Klonopin, Phenobarbital, Ativan and Ambien. Anti-depressants such as Amitriptyline, Pamelor, Trazodone, Prozac, Zoloft, Paxil, Effexor and Remeron. Also, many migraine medications which were introduced after I was deep into my addiction. These truly work for my migraines today without any mood altering effects or possibility for addiction. Those that I've taken include DHE,

Migranal, Midrin, Imitrex, Amerge, Maxalt, Zomig, Relpax, Cafergot, Ergostat, Depakote, Axert, and Topamax, along with anything over the counter you could possibly name. As strange as it may sound I never did a street drug, short of some hits off a joint as a teenager.

The next couple of years at home and work it seemed like life was good again. I was in my early 40's. The doctors were writing prescriptions and the pills were flowing. I had a combination put together by now that really seemed to work. Ultram and Vicoprofen quickly became my two favorite narcotic pain pills. During this first couple of years of popping pills, my family and friends would comment on how good I looked and that I was more outgoing and willing to participate in activities. I was losing weight of course, as I quickly learned the effects of the pills were more intense on an empty stomach. When I discovered Ultram (Tramadol) I truly thought it to be my miracle drug. Ultram was kind of like Stadol. It was introduced as a safer, less addictive pain medication compared to hardcore narcotics, so it was easy at first to get prescriptions for 100 pills at a time. Ultram, unlike its opiate cousins, is a synthetic narcotic created by chemists in a lab. My first 'script for Ultram was for 20 tablets, the prescribed dose being one every eight hours. I took my first tablet, not expecting anything to happen except to give me some headache relief. The pharmacist said it might make me a little dizzy, which was all.

Goodbye Stadol, hello Ultram! I never felt so good and only one pill did this! And long lasting? Fourteen hours later I still had this state of well being going on. I was relaxed and peaceful. My cigarettes tasted better, music sounded better and I could sit through an entire movie and just mellow out. Life seemed good. Little did I realize that this was a false sense of well being that was bringing out this new personality. I kept thinking, would just one pill do this? Not! I'm a drug addict, so if just one made me feel that good what would two or three be like? I also had a lot to learn about tolerance and resistance and how the body builds it up and it keeps taking more and more pills to get that initial high. I was off and running, going nowhere fast.

Soon I was up to five Ultram at a time. I was starting to notice that if I skipped a day or two between refills that I would get physically ill. But after scoring on some more and waiting the 45 minutes I was feeling no pain, just euphoria. The thing about Ultram is it did take some time to kick in, but it was worth the wait as the high lasted many hours longer than other pain pills. This is where I discovered Vicoprofen for that quick high I wanted and then followed up with Ultram for many hours of relief. Yes, Jackie had her times of worry and frustration, but I managed to hide the severity of my growing addiction. Soon I was up to five Ultram twice a day, combined with the Vicoprofen or Percocet and frequent injections of Demerol at the ER or the doctor's office. I quickly learned that Nubain injections were effective, but if I had other narcotics in my system it would neutralize their effects and no high would be obtained. I used to treasure knowledge of sports like boxing, football, basketball, baseball and fishing. My present knowledge became a sick sense of what drugs went together for that constant feeling I craved.

I think I knew I was spiraling out of control as I did with the Stadol, but was powerless to do anything about it. God, who had always been number one in my life, took a backseat to these chemicals. After all, this couldn't be my fault, not with the headaches, anxiety and depression. I deserved to be pain-free and not experience that awful mind-racing. I couldn't cope with life on life's terms anymore, and I wasn't hurting anyone. Or so I thought. Even my occasional prayers to God for help when the withdrawal pains set in, were tainted. Right in the middle of my cries for help I would think of the possibility of a refill the next morning. So I didn't really want God's help, not near as much as my next prescription, that's for sure.

Months soon became years and I found myself deceiving doctors, pharmacists and family to support my habit. That one Ultram tablet that initially made me feel so good had now become an obsession. Ten to 15 pills at a time wasn't uncommon, sometimes twice a day. And, of course, this included many other pain pills, tranquilizers and sedatives. I was put on a drug called Amitriptyline to prevent migraines. Somehow the pharmacist gave me 50 refills. I discovered that taking several of these at a time produced a strange effect in me. I would lie on the sofa and come to 24 hours later. I would randomly speak when I wasn't asked a question. One night, Jackie discovered me sleeping on the toy box in Dani's room. This drug even became too weird for me and I feared doing something under its influence that I would regret the rest of my life.

The prison system is crowded with inmates who were under the influence of drugs or alcohol when they committed their crime. I hope and pray that especially the young people reading this would realize this simple truth; you can do something in an instant that will change your life forever. Something you never would have considered if you hadn't been drunk or high. My own personal list of insanities, all drug related, is long and painful to put down on paper. Please understand that I deeply regret my actions. It is not my intent to sensationalize or stretch the truth in any way. When I inject humor it is only because that is how I deal with it now. And, of course, my sincere amends to the countless people I interfered with just so I could feed my disease. I experienced many so-called 'bottoms' along the way, but the 24/7 constant cravings remained despite my best intentions to recover.

9

To say that I was in denial of my situation is an understatement. My first insanity was the delusion that I could get this under control myself. Countless times I would try and fail in efforts to taper myself off the pills. Either the physical withdrawal pains, which were awful or emotional withdrawal, would do me in. I was so obsessive-compulsive; always counting the pills when returning home from the pharmacy. I would keep a checklist of the number of pills I took each time and invariably dump out the bottle counting again to make sure my count matched what was left in the bottle. Heaven forbid the count would be off, as this would bother me big time. Even when taking a dose I had to be in front of the mirror so I could count the pills on my tongue. One day, doing just this, in front of the bedroom mirror I heard a noise on the dresser as I put the pills in my mouth. Oh no, I must have dropped one! I proceeded to tear the bedroom apart looking for that lost pill. Jackie walked in to find me on my hands and knees, the dresser pulled away from the wall.

"What are you doing?" she said with good humor as she chuckled. But her good mood quickly soured as I told her what

I was in search of; but I finally found those 'spiders' that had been biting me! You see, I'd been itching terribly for some time. It's a result of drug abuse and is commonly referred to as 'bugs under your skin.' Most of my t-shirts had holes in them, as I would grab a fork, knife or scissors and scratch my back. So I proceeded to show Jackie the spiders as I pointed to the bed. They were crawling around on the comforter I told her with conviction. I could see spiders! Very small and a lot of them! I actually became angry with Jackie because she couldn't see them. She left the house in disgust. That had become all to frequent. As she walked out, I returned to my knees, stroking the carpet, looking for that pill that was still hiding from me.

I often times would stuff a piece of paper towel in my pill bottles so they wouldn't rattle around in my pocket. This paranoia also led me to hide my drugs around the house. At work, not only would my locker be secured with a padlock, but also the pills inside would be wrapped in something. Once in a pair of socks, because in my sick mind, life as I knew it would stop if my pills came up missing! I started doing anything to feed my ever-growing addiction. Between refills became my hell on earth. I tried drinking straight vodka or tequila to ease my withdrawal pains, but the effects of alcohol were short lived and didn't do the trick like painkillers, tranquilizers or sedatives.

Looking back, I can see that God intervened or protected me during these insane times. Like the night I went fishing some two hours north of here to one of my favorite fishing holes; popping pills before, while fishing and after. I left for home in the wee hours of the morning. It only took two hours getting there but somehow five hours to get home. I came to, just a couple of blocks from home, without a clue how I had gotten there.

Another all night fishing adventure found Dani, now seven years old, with me. She loved to go fishing with her dad and nighttime angling was even more exciting. Meanwhile, with no regard to Dani's safety I was under the influence of narcotics again. Yes, even the intense high I get from fishing was increased when I had my pills. Dani had retired to the car parked close by to sleep as I fished the night away. When we left at three or four in the morning it was still dark out. The combination of drugs and fatigue was settling in. As I drove down a large hill, know locally as 'Goat Hill' I panicked. As Dani lay in the backseat sleeping with no seatbelt on I saw bright lights in my rearview mirror. A semi was close behind and its bright headlights reflected off a bridge at the base of Goat Hill. In my drug-fogged head I thought I saw an oncoming car headed straight at me. I turned the wheel sharply to avoid the car that existed only in my mind. I narrowly escaped hitting the bridge. Thank you Lord, for watching out for my precious daughter Dani that early morning.

But if nothing changes, nothing changes. Know God, know peace; no God, no peace. When going to a pharmacy to get a refill I would have a water bottle or a soda on the car seat so I could swallow down some relief instantly. For years I had the sick idea in my head about how wonderful it would be to steal drugs from a pharmacy or one of the vans that make the deliveries. Thank God I never crossed that line, but it didn't keep me from fantasizing about all those pain pills in those large containers. I gave away my daughter, Sasha, on her wedding day while I was popping Ultram and Vicoprofen. Then at the reception I washed them down with a good amount of margaritas. I thought at the time that it was the only way I could cope with an event that big.

Since then I have learned of many deaths by people who have experimented with such lethal combinations of drugs and liquor. Another such nightmare occurred on a road trip that included a doctor appointment, pharmacy visit and eventually three 40-ounce bottles of beer, and this time I had firearms and ammunition in the trunk. What's wrong with that picture? You see, Jackie wanted all the guns out the house. Can you blame her? So, in an attempt to do a good deed, I devised a plan that would get me some pain pills and hopefully some cash. I would drive to Spencer to a gun store that purchases used firearms. Before leaving home I made an appointment at a town along the way. As I exited the pharmacy with 24 tablets of Percocet in my pocket I met a friend in recovery who was coming in. I had known Diane for sometime as she also struggled with the pill and alcohol thing.

"What are you doing here?" she asked as we met face to face. There I stood, totally busted, with narcotics in my pocket, three guns and enough ammo in my trunk to start a small war.

"Hi, Diane," I responded.

"How ya doing?" she inquired

"Oh, I'm just making a late delivery," I lied. The distributor that I worked for sold just about anything. Whether she bought it or not and why she was there, I'll never know. Deep down I think we both knew each other's intentions. As the saying goes, 'You can fool the fans, but you can't fool the players.' Diane, just two years older than me, passed away a few months later. One of many hopeless nights alone in her apartment led to pain pill and alcohol induced liver failure. I attended Diane's funeral with many regrets of that day we conned each other and many more missed opportunities after that. Diane once told me, after a Twelve Step Meeting, that we, as prescription drug addicts, always need to upgrade strength and dosage and can never downgrade, meaning that's why the Darvocet and mild pain medicines don't give us that high anymore and why O.T.C. medicines such as Nyquil and cold syrups are like water to us. She hit is right on the button! I wish now that we would have talked about more recovery things of hope and real substance. But one thing I've learned over the years is if you put two recovering pharmaceutical drug addicts in the same room it sounds like a doctor's convention. We compare brand names, strengths and dosages, which quickly become war stories. I try today in recovery to avoid such conversations in memory of Diane. Only by the grace of God am I sitting here at this moment recalling these past events instead of taking my own dirt nap. If I could somehow divert another human being from making that fatal mistake of abusing drugs and alcohol then I guess my past was what God intended it to be. Or, should I say, he may have kept me around to tell my story. So shame on me if I avoid doing just that. Today I have a full and thankful heart despite all the wreckage of my past, and sadly the insanities didn't stop there.

10

They included acts of craziness against my own family; as if they weren't suffering enough just watching me slowly kill myself. One day in a rush to get to the pharmacy for a refill I ran into a snag. I was two dollars short of the amount I needed to pick it up. Upon entering Dani's bedroom after searching the entire house something on her bulletin board caught my eye. There hung a two-dollar bill that her grandfather had given her some time ago. I gave it little thought as I snatched it up. It's all that stood between my pills and me. I would cry many tears in the future at treatment centers over that single act of selfishness. Whenever a mood altering substance would enter our house, no matter who it belonged to, it wasn't safe around me. Of course, this included alcohol and prescription cough syrups. Too many times Dani and Jackie's medicines would fall prey to their father and husband. I would trade their pills for O.T.C. look-a-likes and water down the codeine cough medicines. My daughter and two granddaughters living right next door saw their prescription medicine disappear the same way. I recall after a surgery or painful ailment, that Sasha came home with large amounts of

Vicodin and Hydromophone (Dilaudid). I wandered into her house after a day of fishing and heavy drinking. The afternoon sun, combined with alcohol had given me a headache. I knew she had seen her doctor earlier in the week for some pain. I walked into the kitchen and saw the two brown prescription bottles. I swear I can spot a pill container from 100 yards away. I quickly read the labels, revealing the contents. One was Hydrocodone and the other was a much stronger drug, Dilaudid. I popped a handful of the Vicodin in my mouth and exited my daughter's house.

A short time later I returned, as I just had to try the Dilaudid. It and Oxycontin were the only painkillers I had never tried. So into my mouth went a couple of tablets on top of the four Vicodin and a belly full of beer. Wow! I thought, not only was the headache gone but I felt awesome! So I was off to Sasha's volleyball game on a warm summer evening in the park with Jackie, Dani, and my granddaughters, Kay and Ann. We watched Sasha's team play as I drank more and mellowed out in a euphoric state of mind, not even giving a thought to my condition or the fact that my family was present. Afterward, I got behind the wheel of my car and, no doubt, one of my granddaughters was probably riding home with their grandpa. 'Papa' as they call me, should not have been driving!

In the days that followed I would return to Sasha's home and help myself to her pills. Each time telling myself the lie I had told many times. This is it, no more, these are for Sasha's pain, but I kept going back. Finally I convinced myself that Sasha was feeling better, opening the door to my next insane action. Matching up the Vicodin with an O.T.C. look-a-like was easy. The other drug, the Hydromorphone, the one that I craved most, didn't match anything I could find. Then I discovered they matched my Clonodine, a blood pressure medicine, which, ironically, was prescribed to me to reduce drug cravings. With no regard to the possible danger of Sasha taking these, thinking they were her pain meds, I made the switch. By the grace of God Sasha never took any. In the future, her dad in recovery would tell her of this and other wrongs committed by me against her. Thank you Sasha, for all your love and compassion. I love you.

My oldest daughter, Janna, only lived near us a short time with her husband and our other three grandchildren. For a short time, their home was within walking distance from where we lived. Her husband had just had a minor surgery during this time and he was given a prescription for Tylox, a painkiller with Tylenol and Oxycodone. He may have taken one or two but I helped myself to the rest. To Janna and her husband and my grandchildren, I sincerely apologize for entering your home when you weren't there. I also apologize for betraying your trust as a dad, grandpa and father-in-law by stealing from you. I love you guys. I also need to apologize to my brother-in-law, Tony. I entered your home also while you lived in Spencer. I took, on several occasions, your Phenobarbital that I knew was for your epilepsy. I have no excuse for violating your trust and stealing from you. I am sincerely sorry for my actions.

To my wife, Jackie, I took advantage of your unconditional love many times. So often I interrupted your sleep, your job and your duties as a mother and grandmother when you took me to the emergency room and doctors office countless times. Using you to get what I wanted hurts the most; especially when you suffered physical pains from your own migraines, kidney stones and surgeries. In the beginning most of your pain meds were taken by me and near the end you started refusing them to protect my recovery. For the physical and emotional pain you endured, I am truly sorry. I love you today just as I did some thirty-seven years ago when you first flipped me the peace sign from behind the wheel of your blue mustang. You are truly a saint among women and I thank God for you! To the many doctors, nurses, and pharmacists who in compassion tried to help ease my pain. I ask for your forgiveness also for the many times I conned you for no other reason than to feed my addiction. Even on one Christmas Eve morning I took advantage of your spirit of good will by tampering with my patient chart to get more pain meds. At my lowest point I was working seven different doctors for drugs and all the pharmacies in the area. I thank God for the alert pharmacist who quickly foiled my only effort to forge a prescription.

Even our dog, Rameses, and cat, Pumpkin, weren't spared from my insanities. Rameses returned home from the vet clinic after surgery with painkiller laced dog biscuits. These were eaten by his owner and washed down with a six-pack of beer. Pumpkin was put in a little more dangerous situation as we left for a week's vacation. She had been suffering from frequent seizures until she was treated with Phenobarbital, but one night as we were leaving for a fishing trip in northern Minnesota I thought only of myself. With the long drive ahead I took a look at the bottle of anticonvulsants, opened it and swallowed the contents. Jackie and Dani loved this pet, but as they waited for me in the car I pitched the empty bottle in the garbage can. Our other daughter, and pet caretaker in our absence, would never see the note with instructions to give our cat her pills. I thought the two vials of Nubain and syringes that I had gotten from our doctor wouldn't be enough for such a long trip, and it turned out not to be as we had to stop at two hospital ER rooms along the way for painkiller injections.

I soon discovered that as I continued on this path of destruction the insane actions increased in severity. My constant cravings turned into a hunger not to feel that rarely could be satisfied anymore. I was on that roller coaster of highs and lows. In the beginning of my drug and alcohol use the highs outlasted the lows. That wasn't the case anymore. The lows just kept getting lower. I couldn't even get out of bed anymore; let alone shave, shower and go to my job. I truly was physically, emotionally and spiritually sick. Getting my pills or injections became harder and harder as most everybody had wised up to my bad intentions. My family and work place suffered through my frequent states of withdrawal right along with me. I was just a shell of an employee, husband, father and grandfather. I withdrew from everyone and would actually lose a day once in a while because I slept so much. It was so strange, the fact that when I had pills in my pocket the last thing I cared about was sleep, but 24 hours after they ran out I could never get myself out of bed unless there was a possibility to score some pills. With a supply of pills, life seemed good, but there was always a price to pay when they ran out. In the end that price got too high. Every emotionally and physically painless moment under the influence came back tenfold in the hellish pain of withdrawal. The truth is, I'll always continue to get worse, never better, until I decide to surrender to God and admit my own powerlessness. As kryptonite is to Superman so mind-altering chemicals are to me, but God could and would rescue me if I just surrendered. But it would get darker before I saw the light.

I recall my adventure with triple hernia surgery. I had been around the tables of recovery for some time and knew that there was always 'a way out.' As the surgery approached I pledged to family and friends that I would be honest to doctors, surgeons and nurses about the severity of my addiction. My subconscious mind knew all along that I didn't stand a chance. An entry in my journal, days before my surgery said, in large print, "SCARED SHITLESS." I ignored the smaller entry that said, "Just Pray." Another entry the next day said, "I am what I am. What did you expect?" I went into surgery ten days clean and sober on a whim and a prayer. I failed instantly, afterward accepting and then requesting every injection of Morphine and Demerol they would allow. In the next 12 days after returning home I lied, cheated and deceived my way to get what I craved. One desperate afternoon, I faked falling in the shower, claiming I had re-injured my incisions in an effort to get more pain medicine. The 12 day total reached 160 Vicodin tablets, 80 Percocet and one dangerous afternoon of washing them down with quarts of beer. All I accomplished was to put a damper on our Christmas that year, the last Christmas we would get to spend with Jackies mom who passed away that spring. A couple weeks later an entry in my journal would speak of my state of hopelessness. It reads, "Glad to be back at work, but got freaked out Fri. AM when the demons came calling". What are you going to do for two and a half days? What are you going to do at 11:00 AM when you get off work?" I hate that feeling. A prayer entry went like this, "Dear Lord, please remove my obsession for pills."

To those who know the hurt, the pain, and the struggle; my hope for you, as for me, is that we may find 'victory in the struggle.' We are truly torn between two lovers, two Gods, the God of hope and the god of our disease. Our God of hope and the only true God calls us to repent and go in a different direction. "I am He who will sustain you. I have made you and I will carry you; I will sustain you and I will rescue you." Isaiah 46:4. Contrary to the God of hope is the lower power, the god of hopelessness, of our addiction, that only wants suffering and death for us.

I received a letter during this time from one of the extra doctors I was seeing even though I was court ordered to see only one doctor. The letter read, "12/03/03. Dear Mr. Dryden: I have already been suspecting drug abuse on your part. I found out that you have a very well known history of drug addiction and alcoholism. I will withdraw from your care effective today for any matter involving any type of pain. I will only be available for emergency situations where you are unable to get in touch with your regular medical doctor. Sincerely, Dr. R.O. M.D."

What is it about hospitals, pharmacies, doctors and dentists offices? That smell, the aroma of pharmaceuticals in the air. I realize this to be a random and off the wall statement, but it seems to fit in the middle of these insanities. I can walk into a Wal-Mart or K-Mart and my nose can tell you where the pharmacy is. Jackie thinks I'm nuts and she's usually right.

11

Now it's time for the final acts; the lowest of my lows, the force that began a life of recovery. At the end of my sporadic but heavy drug and alcohol abuse I was becoming delusional and suicidal. I didn't want to die but I couldn't live like this anymore. I would stop at nothing to get just one more pain-killer prescription. I drank and drank more alcohol but craved the pills. One night as I was sleeping alone, I rolled out of bed and cracked my knee against our dresser. Jackie was sleeping in Dani's room. This is the only time I can remember her being so disgusted by my using behavior that she wouldn't even sleep in the same bed as me. So, as I lay there, my only conscious thought was, did I break my knee? Could I be so lucky? In my deteriorating state of mind an injury meant pain meds. So as I slowly stumbled up to see that it was only a scrape, that mechanism in my head started up. You know what mechanism I'm talking about if you're a recovering alcoholic or addict. The mechanism that we were possibly born with or acquired along the path of our drinking and using years. The mechanism in our brain that separates us from the people who can drink or take medicine in moderation. Mine has always seemed to be just a little left of center. Sitting there on the edge of the bed obsessing with the broken knee thing I was still half asleep. All the barbiturates (Fioricet) I took before bed surely didn't help either.

I stumbled to our back porch and pulled a claw hammer out of the tool drawer and proceeded into our living room. As I sat there, hammer in hand; I knew what I had to do. This is it, I'm going to do it, one hard hit would dislocate my knee and off to the ER. Jackie would take me. As I raised the hammer I gave no thought to Jackie and Dani sound asleep in the next room. One time, I kept thinking, one hard swing and it would be over. I did it suddenly, but just before impact I must have held back slightly. My knee held firm but I screamed out something awful. I suddenly realized my family sleeping nearby as I tucked the hammer under my lap. Jackie came running out of the bedroom demanding to know what was wrong. Even with all I'd put her through she kneeled there before me in loving concern. I told her that I fell out of bed and hit my knee on the dresser. As she went to turn on the living room light I looked down at my lap. There was the claw of the hammer sticking out by my crotch! I quickly grabbed a piece of clothing near by and stuffed it between my legs as she returned. As she inspected the self-inflicted damage all she wanted to know was if it was broken. Meanwhile, I'm thinking I have to downplay this and get her back to bed before she discovers the hammer I'm sitting on.

"I'm ok. I'm ok. You go back to bed. I'll put some ice on it. You just go back to bed." If she had discovered the hammer surely I'd be taken to the mental ward. All I really accomplished that night was more family disruption and a terribly swollen and very sore knee.

One lonely night as I was between refills I made a trip to Wal-Mart to pick something up for Jackie. Suddenly there I was in the pharmacy aisle even though they were closed. I'm standing among the liquid cold remedies in plastic containers of blues and reds, greens and yellows. I knew deep down that these wouldn't do anything except make me sick and tired, but even sleeping away my troubles sounded good. So I grabbed a couple of different colors and headed home. Jackie and Dani were watching TV in the other room so I sat in the kitchen and sipped my bright colored syrups while listening to music to fit my 'poor me' mood. You know, something like, "Haven't Got Time for the Pain" by Carly Simon. I took my last swallow and nothing was happening. My own pain wanted something stronger. I was trying to downgrade for a cheap high when I knew that only something 'industrial strength' would do the trick. I went out to the garage and saw some cans of spray paint. I'd heard the stories of those who used this as their drug of choice. How convenient and cheap too, I thought. No doctors, no pharmacies. So in one of those desperate attempts not to feel I grabbed a can of gold paint and a rag. Though I didn't have a clue how to do this or the brain cells to spare, I sprayed the cloth. After several hits all I accomplished was to give myself a headache. On top of that, here came Jackie out the kitchen to give me a kiss goodnight. So what exactly am I going to tell her when she asks why my face smells like paint? I kept my distance to avoid a trip to the fourth floor, the ward of our local hospital, which is where you go when you, well, when you start behaving like I was.

Lies, lies and more lies all goes with the disease. I can recall a time when I was toweling off from a shower. Jackie walked in to get something, took one look at my chest and said, "What are all those white circles?" You see, I had talked the doctor into prescribing me Morphine patches. The proper dose was one patch on your shoulder but that being too obvious I went for my chest and, of course, one is never enough so I put four patches on a couple of days earlier. While I was in the shower I removed them and I didn't look in the mirror as I got out. If I did I would have seen what Jackie did; four white full moons on my chest. I don't recall what lie I told on this occasion, but I'm sure it was a whopper!

As my state of mind started to deteriorate so did the frequency of self-abuse. My past history of cutting myself became even more serious now. One such incident found me lying on our basement floor, hopeless, with a large rock in my hand. I wanted to break something, this time my hand. A couple of hard hits left me only with a severe sprain.

Another day I wanted to go fishing and during the worst of times this wasn't possible without the rattle of a pill bottle in my pocket. After being turned down by my doctor and pharmacy, desperation again set in. I needed a plan and that sick mechanism in my brain again kicked in giving me an instant lift. I would go fishing out of town and inflict some kind of injury and then go to a doctor there for some painkillers. Out of town fishing trips often resulted in me 'fishing for pills' instead of fish. So I arrived at the lake some twenty-five miles away. Depression had set in again something awful. No purpose, no direction, I just wanted that numbness. Fishing had always given me such a natural high, before the age of thirty-eight, that is. Since that time it's been only a false sense of well-being and it never lasts. I walked along the rocky shoreline looking for the spot that was best suited to injure a leg or ankle.

Been there, done that I thought as I wedged my ankle between two very large stones. I picked up a large rock and tried over and over as my heart raced. I couldn't make myself do it, so I settled for a few 24 ounce cans of beer in my car on the way home. No pun intended, but my life was truly resting between a rock and a hard place. I was aimlessly going nowhere, accumulating weeks and months of sobriety only to sell out in a weak moment.

Jackie and I traveled to a near by city during one stretch of sobriety as I held on by a fingernail. As we finished our meal panic set in. The drug dragon came calling with an army of demons. I became obsessed as the painkiller cravings settled into my head. As we exited the restaurant I suddenly grabbed my side.

"What's wrong?" Jackie asked. I doubled over giving my best performance. I told her I thought it was a kidney stone or my appendix or something like that. Whatever it was it was serious! You see, once I get locked in on the idea that I need pain relief there's no stopping me. I would go to any length to get what I wanted. So to the ER we went. Soon I was hooked up to a Morphine drip and the panic subsided. Before being released the next morning I was given what I really wanted; a prescription for Hydrocodone 10's, a potent painkiller and of course I emptied the bottle before the day ended.

One afternoon, after visiting a dear friend in recovery at the hospital I had another moment of insanity. My friend Raymond was in the hospice wing dying of cancer. He had been clean and sober for many years and had helped countless people along the way. Raymond's days on earth with us were growing short. He was in extreme pain, the cancer slowly but steadily taking over. Of course he was being given heavy duty pain medicine and rightfully so. We sat and joked about it as Raymond knew what my drug of choice was. I had been around the tables of recovery for sometime and I thought that joking about it was healthy and healing.

We both laughed as I said to my friend, "Hey Raymond, what are they going to do with all those empty Morphine bottles you got stacked up over there?" I was pretty sure I could still squeeze some out. I recall one of the last things Raymond said to me, "are you gonna chair the meeting tonight Mike?" He wanted to go so bad but was unable to leave the hospital. I spent one of the last nights of his life with him as many others volunteered to do. The nurses appreciated it. Countless friends in recovery stayed overnight or made regular visits. These were very special, caring people as was my friend. I love you Raymond and thanks for loving me. I know we were from two different worlds, you being the biker and me being the fisherman. Trying to stay clean and sober one day at a time brought us together in the beginning and kept us together in the end. You'll be missed here on earth, but rest assured, 'in heaven there is no pain.'

Upon returning home that craving not to feel hit again, so my pattern continued. I made the call and received a prescription for ten Ambien tablets. I took all ten of those strong sleeping pills during the evening and overnight, but safe, restful sleep eluded me. Instead I got weird, really weird! The next morning found me 'cooking' what vaguely resembled scrambled eggs with chunks of raw fish. Dani went in the bathroom with the phone, turned the faucet on so I wouldn't be able to hear and called Jackie telling her that something was wrong with dad. Jackie got on the phone and started calling the doctor and then the police station to please help her out of control husband.

Another plea for help came from my daughter Sasha as I went on a doctor shopping spree. My insane plan on this morning was to see two doctors in town and I made another appointment back in Spencer for a late afternoon appointment. This would be a four hour trip that would most likely find me messed up and behind the wheel. Both of my appointments here in town were with different doctors in the same building, even on the same floor about twenty yards apart. Boy, my brain was really firing on all cylinders that day, not!

I suppose my thought at this time was why make two trips as I scheduled the appointments only a half an hour apart. As doctor number one injected me with Demerol and gave me some sample packets of Ultram I thought all was well. At this point I ran into a snag. You see, to get the Demerol shot I had to agree not to drive home. In the past at other offices I was able to slip out some way or another. Not this time, as they wouldn't let me get out of the chair until I had a driver to pick me up. 'Wow,' I thought, 'they sure know how to ruin my plan!' My next doctor appointment down the hall was in a few minutes and just who could I call to come and get me? The wheels in my head spun to no avail, I was busted! Finally I called Sasha to get the nurses off of my back. Now I just had to come up with a story and it had better be a good one! Sasha arrived and as we exited the doctor's office I told her something to cover my butt. It seemed to be working until we ran into a nurse from doctor's office number two in the hallway. There she stood in the hallway, syringe in hand.

"Oh Mike," she said, "come on in. I just got back from the pharmacy with your pain medicine." What happened next is still fuzzy in my mind. I do know that Sasha talked to the staff in both offices. Angry, embarrassed and apologetic she strongly conveyed to them that her dad has a serious problem. Once again, I had nowhere to hide.

12

My first intervention with some force behind it came from my family doctor. At that time I was refilling my Ultram through a friendly pharmacist for 100 pills most every week. Finally, on one desperate Saturday I got a little pushy and they called my doctor. Jackie and I went to see him and I admitted that I was hooked. I again discovered a wonderful thing called 'tapering off.' After carefully putting together a plan on paper for me to slowly cut back on dosage I perked up. The doctor handed me a prescription for 190 Ultram tablets! These were to be tapered down over the next couple of months. In a perfect world I would follow as directed and when the last pill was taken I'd be drug free. My addiction world was anything but perfect. I didn't even make it through the first day without cheating on my dosage. My theory on tapering off has always been to just feel good now and I'll catch up and redouble my efforts later. As the days went on I kept lowering my magic number. That meant I would keep popping them at my discretion until I had a certain amount left and then 'Dr. Mike' would taper off from there. First it was 150 then 75 and finally the day came when I was down to just 50. 'This is it,' I said to myself, 'I can do this!' But two days later they were all gone. In less than three weeks I managed to take every last one. Panic set in 24 hours later when the pains of withdrawal came calling. If you've ever had the flu take that times ten and this is what drug withdrawal is like.

Jackie, in her compassion, listened to my confession and after seeing me so physically ill went to see the doctor alone. I don't blame him one bit, after being used like that, he had very little sympathy for my situation. He told Jackie something like, 'Mike will just have to ride it out the hard way,' which meant cold turkey, and suggested Twelve Step Meetings. The next couple of weeks were horrible, definitely my bottom. After spending what I thought at the time were the worst two weeks of my life, I returned to work.

As the weeks passed my cravings did not, and of course, there were always those migraines to use as an excuse. Soon I was conning the doctor out of Vicoprofen (Hydrocodone with ibuprofen). After all, the problem was with the Ultram I said as I sat in his office with my head in my hands complaining about my headaches. I started playing the same games with him and the pharmacist for frequent refills of 60 pills. Once again the pharmacy called him with concerns on how fast I was going through the Vicoprofen.

I was sleeping when the doctor called our house and spoke with Jackie. Disgusted, she woke me up and told me the doctor wanted to speak with me. I managed to keep all this from Jackie for the most part but time and time again my sickness resurfaced and I was exposed. Jackie called our oldest daughter over and the two of them proceeded to talk to me. "Michael you need help." "Dad you can't fix this on your own. Please go to a treatment center." At first I balked, but their persistence continued until I finally gave in. The plan was for Jackie to call our doctor and see what he recommended. His first choice was a 30 day in-patient treatment center only 20 minutes away. "That's way too close," I said, trying to protect my reputation. So we agreed that I would go to Omaha, Nebraska, some 100 miles away, to a hos-pital based center there. I was accepted and would leave in a couple of days. I somehow scored a few pills and unbeknownst to Jackie, took them all the morning we left for Omaha.

When we arrived at the hospital, I filled out the paperwork. We soon found out this wasn't a 30 day inpatient program, it was a fourth floor detox containment with limited drug counsel-ing and 12 step meetings. They agreed to keep me for a week to 10 days and taper me off the pills. You heard it right, here we go again! Of course I was elated to here this. I sat there in the administrations office excited as she phoned around trying to get me Methadone treatment. My bubble quickly burst when she found out that Methadone wasn't used in Nebraska anymore. She did find a doctor that would detox me with Valium and Lortab (Hydrocodone). My spirits lifted again and I eagerly asked when we could get started.

Now this is my kind of treatment center, I thought as I envi-sioned lying in a hospital bed, watching TV and being given Lortab and Valium. My highly anticipated euphoria was quickly deflated as they strip searched me for any drugs I may have smuggled in. This certainly wasn't the hospital I had expected; it looked more like a mental ward. More like drug treatment with-out the frills of just a stay in the hospital. I was quite scared as Jackie and Dani left and returned home.

The nurse, seeing my panic and anxiety, offered me Valium and I took all that she would allow. As soon as she could get a hold of the doctor the Hydrocodone treatments would start.

Needless to say, I was comforted to hear this! Recovery from drugs and alcohol is only successful when an individual wants it more than anything else and is willing to go to any length to get it. I've heard it said that to get to a place we've never been, we must follow a path we've never taken. Looking back, I can see that I wasn't ready to surrender totally or to admit my own powerlessness. In treatment centers there are positive and negative forces just as there are in the outside world. We have the choice to choose and to follow either one. One of God's greatest gifts to mankind may be that of individual free will. Without it we would just be robots programmed to do whatever our higher power wanted of us. If we hadn't been blessed with freewill there would be no merit in choosing good over evil. We were not created to wander aimlessly without any purpose.

I witnessed both positive and negative forces here in my first real rehab. My roommate about half my age made it quite clear to me that he wasn't ready for a life change. War stories told by people in rehab can be very damaging to them and those that listen. There is a big difference between a healthy cleansing of the soul and the bragging and false pride connected to war stories. This young man told me things I didn't need to know. In one such story he stated that he got high on over the counter cold medicine. He went into great detail about the right brand to get and the effect he experienced. That was too much information for me as I've always searched for something O.T.C. other than alcohol that would numb my feelings. I also learned from him that not only did Hydrocodone come in stronger doses but certain pharmaceutical brand names were better than others. That warped mechanism in my head feeds on information like this. It's definitely on a need-to-know basis and it doesn't need to know this!

This kind of information creates even more conflict for the stories of hope that my heart craves. I remember playing cards with two gentlemen one night and on our table was an Omaha World Herald newspaper. An ad for a local casino grabbed our attention as we all noticed the bold print exclaiming Wednesday nights as Margarita Discount Night. We all decided that we ought to meet there some Wednesday after we get out and have margaritas. I really don't think we realized at the time the insanity of such a statement. Here sat three grown men living on borrowed time, by the grace of God, a prescription drug addict, an alcoholic and a cocaine addict. Such conversation proved our denial to the fact that any and all mood altering substances were like poison to us. A drug, is a drug, is a drug; a hard fact for many to face. Jackie and Dani made the long drive that weekend to join us for a family group session. This was my first honest look at how I had interfered with their lives. Dani, only nine at the time, bless her heart, sat and comforted a little girl whose dad was just being admitted. There was another painkiller addict who attended our session. His drug of choice was Percocet. After that meeting he told me that he had heard about an over-the-counter painkiller called Pergesic. 'Ya know Mike; I heard if you take enough of these you can get the same effect as Percocet.' So much for all the hope my heart was filled with from the meeting. My head got involved again, thinking it may have found an 'ace in the hole.'

Two days before I left, my system was narcotic free. Before leaving for home my doctor told me he couldn't send any pain pills home with me. Ya think!? After all, I was leaving drug treatment for a life of recovery wasn't I? Out patient treatment was recommended at a recovery center close to our hometown. Jackie and I stopped there only to find out it would be very expensive. "I can do this by going to meetings," I told her. After all, 12 step groups are free, but they can't help you if you don't go. My attendance was spotty at best. At first I was like a kid in his first candy store, gathering up all I could. My heart was like a sponge to this thing called spirituality. As soon as my heart would grasp this hope my head would interfere. The constant cravings would continue and soon I would seek out what my head wanted. These meetings showed me there was life after drugs and alcohol and a good life at that, but soon I was attending the meetings under the influence of narcotic painkillers. I wanted the hope that was in my heart but the mechanism in my head craved the numbness. I couldn't completely surrender to facing life on life's terms. It was one step forward and then two steps backward. I wasn't being honest with the guy in the mirror.

13

Michael George Dryden. September 17, 1953—May 4, 1999. Without the grace of God this is how my tombstone would have read. It was a cool, crisp, beautiful, sunny spring morning. Some months earlier I thought I had hit the painkiller jackpot. I started seeing a new doctor and the pills were flowing. He wrote me prescriptions for quantities I had only dreamed of before. Ultram, Tylox, Ativan and Phenobarbital along with office injections of Demerol, but I could soon wear out the patience of even the most generous prescription writers. The more they gave me the more I took. The more I needed the more desperate I became. I hadn't been working for a while but I promised Jackie that I would return soon. When black Monday was just a week or so away I panicked. I was almost out of pills and I had just refilled them all ten days ago. I couldn't go back to work next week without my pills. I'd be too sick to get out of bed, let alone showered and dressed. I needed a plan.

What happened next was a sad excuse for an addict trying to survive just a few more days. I would go see this doctor, crying real tears, and I'd say, "Please help me. I've become addicted to the pills you've been giving me." I had done this many times with many physicians. I would confess to taking too many and ask for his help. Deep down inside I always believed that this was it. I was going to do it right this time. That lie my head told my heart so many times when I thought I wanted to taper off and stop this madness. This doctor not only agreed to my taper off plan, he gave me substantial quantities of 30 milligram Phenobarbital tablets, Ativan and, of course, what I craved the most, a painkiller called Tylox (Tylenol with Oxycodone). I walked out of the pharmacy that day in a euphoric state of mind once again. I had what I wanted and needed for now. It was like the future would never show its ugly head again. It almost didn't.

Time seemed to stop for me when I was handed a prescription, all was well for that moment. On the Friday before my fatal Monday my son-in-law announced he had a big surprise for me. He and I would be going to a nearby city for a professional boxing match. My oldest daughter and him had purchased the tickets some time ago. They knew I was a huge boxing fan. I had just scored on all those pills so of course I wanted to go. So as Tyler drove the two and a half hours I popped pills and pretended all was well. We arrived early so we could visit a riverboat casino first. I had 50 dollars in my pocket that Jackie had given me to enjoy that special night. Gambling is just one more thing that renders me powerless and out of control. I fed the slot machines while Tyler was nearby. Soon I found myself alone and that mechanism in my head took over. You can't win if you don't play. I went for instant gratification, not really caring that I would need some food and drink money at the boxing match.

I once went to a casino with my middle daughter for an evening of enjoyment. I ruined that night also as my total powerlessness was exposed. I started with $175 and four hours later had $1,400. Most people would stop right there and buy their daughter a fancy meal and stay at a nice motel for the night. Maybe some shopping the morning after and return home all smiles. That was not to be as I quickly discovered that alcohol and drugs weren't the only kryptonite to this superman. Looking back I can see that I was powerless to stop feeding the slot machines. If you have this disease you know what I mean. Some ten hours later found us tired, depressed and penniless. I felt ashamed, embarrassed and pitiful. Our only resources were Sasha's drained checkbook and the gas in her car. The drive home was something I'll never forget and I haven't gambled since that night.

Back to my night of fun with my son-in-law. Tyler soon found me at a slot machine and asked me how I was doing. I told him I thought I probably broke even. I was lying through my teeth. I didn't even have enough for a soda and popcorn at the match. Tyler bought some snacks for himself, each time asking me if I wanted anything. Each time I told him that I was fine. Yeah, I was F.I.N.E. Frustrated, insecure, neurotic, and emotional. Our night of male bonding ended with Tyler driving us home as I swallowed more pills and floated around in never-never land.

Saturday and Sunday found me on our sofa, watching TV, popping pills and fading in and out of consciousness. I woke up Monday around three AM and it hit me that I couldn't go to work. After all, I barely had enough pills left for the week and then what? I knew I was up against a huge barrier and I just didn't want to think about it right now. I went into the living room; I put in the movie Fargo and proceeded to take pills. Lots and lots of pills. I only recall the first part of the movie and nothing after about five AM, the rest has been told to me by

Jackie. She woke up about seven and there I sat a pathetic sight, curled up in a blanket.

"You're not going to work are you?" Jackie asked. I shook my head, "Well you've run out of options, you're going to treatment." "Tell your Dad goodbye," she told Dani, as she left for school. I looked at Dani for what could have been the last time and slurred, "Swing the bat good." I must have thought she was going to softball practice, not to school. What a tragic way to remember what could have been our last time together. Jackie took Dani to school and not wanting to return home went to our oldest daughter's house. I continued taking pills with no sense of reality, only delusions. Our daughter was leaving to go shopping two hours away and Jackie decided not to go with her, reluctantly returning home.

This was the difference, the divine intervention. Without Jackie and God my grave marker would have that day's date on it. May 4, 1999. I could easily write another book just on the things I would have missed out on in the last eight years. Thank you Lord for putting Jackie in my life.

As she entered the house I was laying facedown on the living room floor. In my stupor and utter state of desperation I had finished all three bottles of medicine, the rest of the Tylox, Ativan and Phenobarbital. When I started at three AM there were close to 50 pills in those three bottles. I had apparently stumbled around, breaking things around our house and my big toe before I went down. Jackie called 911 fearing that it was already too late. The police arrived first and discovered that I was unconscious and breathing very shallow. An ambulance arrived next to save my life. There were three empty pill bottles on the coffee table but I had peeled the labels off them. My favorite drug blanket that I was always covered up with had cigarette butts in it so on top of everything else I could have burned our house down!

Off to the emergency room I went where our long time family doctor and close friend tried frantically to revive me. The pills I took weren't prescribed by him so he ordered a tox screen to see what kind and how many pills were in my system. After about 14 hours of fading in and out I woke up in the ICU. There I lay at three A.M., 24 hours after I began my pill marathon. I was confused and angry, hurting physically, mentally and spiritually. I made several phone calls to Jackie, waking her up and being a real jerk. The gratitude I should have shown her gave way to anger. In my state of mind she had overreacted and made a big deal out of nothing. I thought I would have been just fine.

Sadly, I still wasn't ready to admit my powerlessness and surrender myself to God. I was taken up to the fourth floor of our hospital for detoxification and therapy. I was seeing a psychiatrist and soon started working him for Methadone and Klonopin. I spent the rest of the week in a fog. I was ordered to attend outpatient drug treatment and this time I carried through with it. As I went to my counseling sessions I started to realize what I had done. The overwhelming realization hit me that I should have died from my overdose. I was on a natural high for a couple of weeks. I started exercising and taking long walks around the lake. As I approached 30 days of sobriety I began to forget the miracle God had bestowed on me.

14

Life, with all its problems and temptations, soon turned my spirit negative, doubtful and angry. One day as I was walking around the lake my heart wasn't filled with gratitude, it was hurting. That mechanism kicked in and I started lying to myself again. Thoughts of an injection of narcotics soon began ever so lightly, like a kitten, but it was the drug demon in disguise. One frustrating day I picked up a stick as I was walking. Mike, still a prisoner of his fears, resentments, guilt, shame and remorse was a walking time bomb. Before long I started taking swipes at my arm with the stick. Soon there was blood and I felt at ease, not peace, just a poor substitute. Often times, if not always, my behavior turns negative first, then the self-abuse follows and alcohol and drugs are the end result. I soon gave into the headache excuse and went to the doctor for a shot of Nubain. I didn't even make it 30 days after my near death experience and my disease was off and running again. Truly my self will ran rampant, abusing the free will that God has granted us all. The right to make choices.

I continued to attend 12 step meetings and played husband, dad, grandpa and employee but I wasn't being honest with myself. I recognized the seriousness of my situation but was powerless to do anything about it. I didn't want to live like this anymore, was always at battle with the fact that I didn't want to die.

I soon resumed playing the doctor/pharmacy game to get more and more pills and injections. Both my hips became so saturated with old injection sites that calcium deposits began to form. This made it harder and harder to get an effective shot. Like the song says, "Hips don't lie," and mine sure didn't. I was driving out of town to an assortment of doctors and pharmacies just to support my habit. The noose kept getting tighter and tighter until I was busted again and it was time for another intervention. I ended up calling the shots on this one too as I had been seeing a private behavioral counselor. I was sent to this individual by the psychiatrist who saw me after my overdose. I remember I was hurting so bad during these sessions and was often breaking down into tears. This didn't just happen at his office either. I remember taking Dani to school and then crying all the way home. I wanted out of this trap but it truly seemed hopeless. I told him about my addiction and of course my frequent headaches. Then he said something that set me free to use again. It wasn't so much what he said but how I chose to use it.

"Mike," he said, "I believe you need to take care of the physical pain you have before tackling your addiction." To this day I don't think any doctor, counselor, psychiatrist, nurse or specialist understood the severity of my addiction; that if I was left on my own I would have drugged myself to death. Only other recovering addicts understand that warped mechanism in my head. The one that craved numbness, not reality. So the wheels in my head spun until a plan came to mind to please those around me. As always, that plan has something in it for me.

You see, through the years doctors have been recommending that I admit myself into the Diamond Headache Clinic in Chicago. This clinic was considered by many to be the finest in the world. Jackie and our family doctor were all for this as I knew they would be. I was already on short-term disability from work because my psychiatrist ordered it for my severe depression. This gave me an excuse to seek out and take all the painkillers I could get until my trip to Chicago. When I told a variety of doctors my situation and the exact date of my admission they weren't stingy with the prescription pads. Soon we were off for Chicago, stopping in Davenport to see our oldest daughter. I was popping pills along the way; I even visited the ER in Davenport for a shot of narcotics. I was in my comfort zone and it was all about me.

That evening, after my shot for the road (20 mg. of Nubain), we continued on our way. It was dark and Jackie was doing her best to get us to Chicago. Meanwhile, I was having a fit because my latest concoction of drugs wasn't working. The Nubain works great only if you have no drugs in your system, and if you do as I did, popping pills all day, it just erases any kind of high. So there I sat, in my own manufactured crap, making the trip miserable for Jackie and Dani.

We arrived in Chicago later that evening as Jackie persevered, finally getting to the Diamond Headache Clinic. God blessed us with a room right next to the clinic even though we had no reservations. The next morning found us all in better moods as my pills were working again. We treated ourselves to a little sightseeing and then it was back to the clinic. After getting me checked in Jackie and Dani returned home. I was kept there for 12 days, a long and lonely 12 days.

I was soon comforted to discover that, once again, I would be tapered off all the narcotics I was on. The tapering off was short lived and in three or four days they were down to what they do best. One specialist after another diagnosed my headaches. There were classes, therapy sessions and speakers, all focused on my migraines. They tried to teach me relaxation through meditation exercises. A variety of new drugs were introduced, including two a drug addict shouldn't have. I was given a prescription for Klonopin and an injectable muscle relaxant.

Once again, even after me telling them my history, they weren't equipped to deal with my severe pharmaceutical addiction. I was in a state of fog and withdrawal all 12 days and retained very little of what they taught me. In the end I was classified just as I was in Sioux Falls, South Dakota. I was told that I was a classic migraine sufferer with a variety of other headache symptoms. One such expert even told me that occasionally I might need a shot of Demerol to break a headache cycle. This opened the door in my addictive brain, and sadly, that was all I really walked away with from this highly regarded and expensive clinic.

Jackie and Dani arrived to take me home, once again with high expectations. I quickly dampened their enthusiasm. They wanted to spend the day in Chicago and visit the Field Museum. Dani wanted to see the bodies of the Lions of Tsavo from one of her favorite movies. As we pulled into the parking lot I was feeling physically weak to say the least. I felt worse after 12 days in medical care than I did before. I know my body was still in withdrawal and I couldn't pull myself together to even get in and out of the car; let alone spend the entire afternoon walking around the museum. Because of my condition we passed on the visit and left the parking lot to return home. Dani was in tears and I felt awful. I carried the weight of this guilt, shame and remorse for years after. We were in the parking lot, just a walk away from a dream of hers. I wasn't well and it's nothing less than a tragedy that a family should suffer like this because of an alcoholic or an addict.

The quiet trip home was interrupted as I faked a serious migraine to numb my guilty feelings. After 12 days in one of the finest clinics in the world I was back at it. As Jackie looked for an exit to a hospital along the way I tried to cover my denial.

"You know," I said to them, "one of the specialists there told me this might happen and I would need a shot." What was Jackie to do, but trust the man she had loved for so many years? We arrived at an emergency room where I was injected with narcotics and at least I was comforted for the remainder of the trip home.

15

The next morning we awoke to the news that Sasha had given birth to a daughter, Kay. We were off to the hospital to see our new granddaughter. I was having trouble coping as the shot had long worn off and I had no pills other than the Klonopin and the muscle relaxant. There I stood again as husband, dad and grandpa and instead of celebrating this special time in our lives I was drowning in hurt and self-pity. Sasha was given a pain reliever prescription for Tylox no less. Sasha asked me if I would go fill it for her. Jackie, taking one look at the pathetic expression on my face told Sasha that she would go and get it. It was a beautiful day and I suggested that Dani join me for a walk around the lake. Jackie, seeing that I needed to get away, agreed, as did Dani. Our walk around the lake only reached a few hundred feet and I was physically spent. Dani said she understood as we got back in the car. I dropped her off at Sasha's house where Jackie was already. I said I was going home to take a nap. It wasn't sleep that I craved though; instead I wanted to numb my feelings. So there I sat in our basement injecting myself first with the muscle relaxant and then popping several of the Klonopin.

Tranquilizers aren't exactly my drugs of choice, but they would have to do. Wanting quick results I soon swallowed 10 to 15 of the Klonopin tablets. Before they even had a chance to kick in I was on the phone to an out of town doctor's office. I was granted 60 Ultram and 30 Vicoprofen that were called into a pharmacy 25 miles away. I was flying high again as I couldn't leave the house fast enough to go get two of my favorite pain-killers, little realizing or caring that I had a belly full of tranquil-izers which were just starting to show their impact on my consciousness. I arrived at the pharmacy a short time later pick-ing up the pills and purchasing a soda to wash them down. Before I even pulled away in my car I quickly took six tablets of each of the Ultram and Vicoprofen. I started for home only to see this painkiller cocktail turn on me. I was about half way from home and anticipating sitting in the basement and escap-ing one last time.

It was insane to drive a vehicle under these conditions but I just wanted to get home to my sanctuary and be at peace, and then it all started. Suddenly I couldn't stay awake. I fought it frantically, knowing I just had a few more miles to go. It was overtaking me and I couldn't stay in my lane on the highway so I slowed down. This didn't help either as I had short blackouts and would awaken to the sound of rocks pelting against the floorboard. I was over the center line often, jerking the wheel to correct my position. I would hear tires screeching as I would come to and see that my Topaz was all over the road. About this time someone behind me with a cell phone called a nearby highway patrolman. Just five miles from home I met that patrol-man and instantly came of out my stupor, only to see him make a u-turn and turn on his flashing lights. As I pulled over I fumbled around trying to gather the pill bottles off of the seat and put them in the glove compartment. He approached my window and told me a concerned citizen called 911 because they had witnessed me driving out of control and crossing the centerline several times. I wanted out of this situation so bad but I knew I was in trouble. I apologized, telling him I just came from the doctor for a medical condition and must be having a reaction to the medication. He phoned the doctors office to confirm my story, but didn't count the pills left in the bottles. I thought I had dodged a bullet and would soon be on my way. He cited me for crossing the centerline and some other minor infraction, but instead of sending me on my way he phoned Jackie to come and drive the car and I home. Even in my semi-conscious state I knew the shit was going to hit the fan! Only two days home from Chicago and Sasha having just given birth to our granddaughter, Jackie didn't need this. She would have been justified to have the patrolman throw my butt in jail. The first thing she did after he gave her the bottles of pills was to tear them open and scatter them in a nearby ditch. It was a five mile drive home that seemed like 50. I tried to break the silence only once, quickly realizing I had screwed up one too many times.

As she dropped me off at the house she told me that it was over and she didn't care what I did. I remember sitting down on the sofa, the same sofa I had almost died on five months earlier. There I sat a pitiful sight for sure, closing my eyes and passing out. I came to about 12 hours later still sitting in the same spot, in the same position. About this time Jackie's dad walked in and I was welcomed back to reality. He looked at me, and said, "Oh, you're still here," and walked out. My first thought was, 'what have I done?' I completely shattered the trust and hopes of my family. A family that, just weeks ago, embraced my decision to go to a clinic for help; a family that had been excited to pick me up there, after being apart for 12 days. My daughter had just given me a new granddaughter a couple of days ago. I hated myself at that point as my emotions turned to wailing out loud and intense sobbing. That guilt, shame and remorse was back! This time it was crippling. For the first time in years the pills weren't my primary concern. If they were I would have been five miles away on my hands and knees sifting through that ditch. I didn't know what to do. If there was such a thing as hitting rock bottom I felt like I was a foot below that. I would have chose death over this hurt. I tried all day to fix things but no one would listen, it seemed that no one cared. I didn't blame them at all. Soon my hurt turned to anger at myself for what I had done. In an effort, maybe to redeem myself, I started to clean the house. As I did the dishes with trembling hands, one of Jackie's good plates shattered in the sink. As I looked at the broken pieces my self-worth dropped below zero. Picking up a sharp chunk of plate I cut my right forearm and watched myself bleed.

In my emotional coming-down-off-drugs state of mind, I came up with my final plan. Off to the store I went, purchasing a fifth of tequila and a six-pack of beer. My plan un-folded as I took shots of tequila chased with beer. I would finish off all the alcohol that sat before me, then off to the ER for a shot of narcotics. I told myself that after leaving the hospital I would get into my car and drive until I saw a bridge. If I was messed up enough by then and had no fear I would crash my Topaz into the bridge, ending the life I had so screwed up, but God intervened once again as I left the house in the pouring rain. My tequila bottle sat on the table, still half full as I wanted my injection more than the rest of the liquor. As I backed out of the driveway I was met by another car, blocking my way.

Elijah sat under a broom tree. And he asked that he might die, saying, "It is enough; now, O Lord, take away my life, for I am no better than my fathers,"

And he lay down and slept under a broom tree. And behold, an angel touched him and said to him, "Arise and eat." 1 Kings 19:4-5

16

The car in front didn't move and as the door opened my sister got out. My brother-in-law and best friend was behind the wheel. I hadn't seen them in a long time and here suddenly they appeared like two angels.

"Where ya going, Mike?" my sister asked. I slurred out something about having a headache and going to the hospital. They insisted on taking me if I would leave my car at home. We arrived at the emergency room and I attempted to deceive the doctors and nurses, but as I sat on the edge of the ER bed my sister had other plans. She informed the staff of my situation so they knew what they were dealing with. As the doctor came to my bedside I quickly found out it wasn't my will anymore but that of a higher power. Oh yes, I pleaded my case trying to get the magic injection, but to no avail. As I sat there, beaten at my own game, many emotions started coming out. I remember something the ER doctor said to me that night. I had never met him before and all he knew about me was that I was hurting extremely bad.

He then said, "Mike, listen to me. It's always the darkest before the light comes." The next thing I remember is being escorted to a nearby treatment center by a local Deputy Sheriff. It seems that my family doctor and sister signed the papers to have me court committed. They quite possibly saved my life that rainy, hopeless night.

It was just after midnight when I walked those dreaded flights of stairs to the treatment floor with a deputy by my side. I was truly a beaten soul and an emotional wreck as I was checked in and put to bed. The next morning I awoke scared and very depressed. One of the first things I did was call Jackie and tell her I had put myself in here for help. A bit of a lie, but I just wanted her forgiveness to gain a glimmer of hope. Her response was rather cold as she had her fill of my out of control behavior.

My first five days here barely started to clear the fog from my head. I was put on a light dose of Ativan just to control my severe depression as I cried uncontrollably and couldn't eat anything. I called Jackie to see if she would come visit me and bring some clothes.

"Yeah," she said, "I'll throw some things in a garbage bag," I sank deeper into hopelessness at the tone of her voice. A voice once so loving and supportive had now grown weary and cold. As hard as I tried to place blame somewhere else it always came back to the guy in the mirror. I knew where it started and it would have to end with me and me alone, but to totally surrender and admit my personal powerlessness still eluded me.

I called my sister and tried to downplay what had happened. My court appearance was coming and I wanted to fix this and get out of here. Jackie came to my hearing and greeted me with separation of marriage papers. I pleaded with the judge, if he set me free I would clean up my act. The judge asked where I intended to live if he were to dismiss my court committal for treatment. I said I would attend outpatient counseling and hoped to live at home with Jackie and Dani. The judge looked at my wife of so many years as she shook her head and said no.

At this point I reached the depths of self-pity, painfully discovering that I wasn't in control of my destiny. I sat there, a shell of a man, awaiting word from the sheriff's office of where I would be sent for treatment. He approached Jackie and me, telling us I would be taken 60 miles away to a state funded center for up to 30 days. So after 12 days in Chicago and five days at a local treatment center I sat in the back of a sheriff's car again. The ride there found me in my head full of regrets and a broken spirit. A future that seemed bleak and lonely. My life had become unmanageable, I needed help.

I spent three weeks here at inpatient treatment. I lived for the ten minute smoke breaks every hour. My first three days were awful. I was confused and disoriented to say the least. I avoided emotions, even while reading the separation of marriage papers. I had little clothing and couldn't make a phone call for three days. I even feared taking a shower because of my scars from cutting myself. After three days of not taking a shower and having no hygiene supplies a counselor approached me.

"Mike," she asked, "are you showering everyday? How about clothes? We have some extra left behind by other patients." This explained why people seemed to be keeping their distance. You talk about a humbling experience as I had always been quite self-conscious when it came to personal hygiene. The fact was that I had given up and was just hanging on, not eating and not sleeping. I asked the counselor if I could call Jackie for clothes and supplies. I was scared to call her after receiving the papers. I'm sure my ego and pride were getting in the way also. There I sat, in my own misery, phone in hand, wondering how bad my odor really was and 'oh my god, I'm going to have to take the dreaded shower.' I called Jackie and after three days of no contact she sounded concerned and glad to hear from me. This brought on my first tears, opening the floodgate to follow in the next couple of days. Jackie said that she and Dani would bring the things I needed. It was Sunday, visiting day, and they agreed to spend some time with me. My counselor, of course, was glad to here they were coming.

"Now go take a shower," she said with a smile. This lady, who was kind of tough on me at first, has become a close friend of mine in recovery through the years. So off to the shower I went, looking at my scarred arms and fresh cuts on my wrists, only a week old. You must understand that this treatment center was right across the street from the state mental hospital. Surely if the staff here saw the cuts and scars they would lock me up and throw away the key! So I kept these self-inflicted injuries to myself the whole time. A big mistake on my part as one of my counselors became suspicious of my secrets.

"Mike," he said in a soft, caring voice, "if you only reveal 50 percent of your troubles I can only help you 50 percent, but I promise you, if you share 100 percent of your personal stuff I will give you 100 percent of my best problem solving." I shared everything during my stay here, except for the body carvings and the night I lost my virginity. That was an especially ugly experience when I was 15 or 16 in an apartment where two older men resided. Alcohol was involved as well as a willing, older and more experienced woman. I sat there scared to death as the two men took turns having intercourse with her. I wanted nothing more than to just get out of there.

"Mike," they said, "it's your turn." May God forgive me as I caved to the peer pressure and my own personal curiosity. Although this young lady was willing and accepted my advances I felt dirty and disgusting afterward. This one event changed my life forever and I carried tremendous guilt, shame and remorse for years. As I write this now it is the first time I've ever shared it. Not even Jackie knew until reading this.

I realize now after hundreds of meetings, several treatment centers and many relapses that I must clear away the wreckage of my past. For me, a life of sobriety and peace depends largely on this. It's really quite sad that I carried this stuff around so long, trying to numb its existence with alcohol and painkillers. I could never find true peace. So on a Sunday afternoon Jackie and Dani came to visit. I couldn't hold back the tears. When it came time for them to leave I just wanted to go home with my family. The next few days in treatment I broke down in group and shared many of my hurts. I sobbed so violently at times that my counselor had to console me and told me take a deep breath. I swear the carpet in that room is still wet from the tears that poured out. I kid you not, my first two weeks were nothing but painful. I tried everyday to get out of there. In my confused thinking I needed to get home and fix things. No surprise, I had been a quitter my whole life, why would this be any different? About this time I received a letter from Dani who was only ten years old at the time. The letter read as follows:

Dear Dad, I really miss you, but I want you to stay your 30 days and get better. I believe you can get better. I'm bringing you a present on Sunday when I come. I can't wait until you get home. Mom says you can come for Christmas. You can see my report card on Sunday. Mrs. B says I'm doing really good. The weather is really nice here. My hedgehogs are really cute. Their names are Sydney (1) and Gena (6).

After reading this special letter from our miracle child I committed to graduating from treatment. Alcoholism and drug addiction are family diseases and they were hurting too. Dani even had to see a counselor at school to get through this. Jackie was put on Prozac for her own depression. My counselor told me something that I really believe to be true. He said that depression is nothing more than tons and tons of sadness. Jackie and Dani attended family group therapy with me once a week. I remember my counselor asking Jackie, "So what's it like living with Mike?"

She responded that the first 16 years were wonderful but the last eight or nine have been a nightmare. This was exactly the time my pharmaceutical addiction took control of my life. Meanwhile I attended two groups a day, most everyday, searching for answers when I didn't even know the questions. My mind was racing so bad I could only get two or three hours of sleep a night. I would wake up hours before anyone else and sit on the edge of my bed. I was so homesick and worse than that I couldn't even return home when I got out. Jackie requested that we live apart for six months and then see if she and I were ready. I remember that my chore in treatment was to clean the bathroom toilets. As I bent over one of the stools I thought that maybe I needed to stoop this low. From down here I could possibly make the climb back up the ladder of life. Naps and time in front of the TV were seldom allowed here. Every minute of your time was scheduled and you were expected to be on time for every activity. One of my assignments for group was to make a list of interferences, resentments, unmanageables, insanities, gratitude, avoidance of feelings, who is Mike, and perfectionism. The following pages will reveal exactly what I wrote down for these, starting with how I interfered with peoples lives.

Interferences...

I interfered in the life of Jackie when I was pulled over by a highway patrolman. I interfered in the lives of my sister and brother-in-law by threatening suicide. I interfered in the life of Jackie by lying about abusing painkillers. I interfered in the life of Dani by being too weak from withdrawal to join in her activities. I interfered in the life of my supervisor by missing work because of opiate withdrawal. I interfered in the life of Jackie by my lack of companionship. I interfered in the life of Jackie by my neglect as a husband and father forcing her to file for separation papers after 27 years of marriage.

I interfered in my own life by turning to painkillers in times of need instead of trusting God. I interfered in the life of my doctor by calling him at home for painkillers. I interfered in the life of my granddaughter, Ann, by being too weak to carry her on my shoulders when she asked me to. I interfered in the life of Dani by sitting on the sofa in a state of sedation instead of having conversation or playing games with her. I interfered with the safety of others by getting behind the wheel of a car. I interfered with the work performance expected of me at my company by my use of painkillers. I interfered in the lives of my family by overdosing on painkillers. I interfered in my life by not taking better care of myself physically.

I interfered in my life by my lack of faith in God. I interfered in the life of my mother by stealing her prized coin collection. I interfered in the life of Jackie by my doctor bills. I interfered in the life of my father-in-law by my poor income and doctor bills.

I interfered in the lives of my family by my many detoxes and drug treatments.

Resentments...

I resent the fact that I have headaches. I resent the fact that I'm not with my family. I resent the fact that I'm not at work. I resent the fact that I thought about me so much and not about my family. I resent the fact that I've been self-centered. I resent the doctors that gave me so many pain pills and shots. I resent the fact that I feel like crap. I resent the fact that I haven't had an appetite in weeks. I resent the fact that I won't let go and let God. I resent the pharmacies for giving me early refills. I resent the fact that I turned to painkillers instead of God. I resent my drug abuse.

I resent being filled with self pity. I resent going to the headache clinic in Chicago. I resent ever using painkillers. I resent the fact that I can't sleep. I resent the fact that I've slowed down so much in thinking, processing and absorbing. I resent the fact that I was served separation papers from my family.

Unmanagables...

Having headaches. My addiction to painkillers. My wife serving separation papers. Being court committed to in-patient. Being gone from work. Feeling sad. Being arrested for vandalism as a teenager. My time spent in county jail as a teenager. My family moving to Utah. Missing out on walleye fishing in October. My father-in-law loosing respect for me. Not seeing my daughters right now. Not graduating from high school. My brother going to Vietnam. My mom and dads divorce. My last trip to the pharmacy. Being pulled over for driving high. When I feel angry at work. My doctor bills. My family's hurt feelings. My family's lack of trust in me. Being arrested for reckless driving.

My father being an alcoholic. My father passing away. When I'm mad at myself. My daughter getting pregnant at fifteen. My daughter going into treatment. My brother's divorces and drinking. Wanting my marriage fixed right now. Wanting myself fixed right now. Wanting to be home with my family. When I feel mad about what I've done. Two of my daughters not graduating high school. My long hours at work and its affect on my family. Missing our daughter's school activities. My daughter running away on mother's day. My daughter using alcohol and drugs.

My daughter's male dependency. Dani being born with pneumonia causing physical problems. Missing opportunities to show affection to Jackie. My family being sad that I'm gone. Missed opportunities to be a better husband to Jackie.

Insanities...

Abusing painkillers. Stealing from my daughters. Lying to my wife. Still using after three detox's. Using after out patient treatment. Using drugs after an overdose. Using drugs after being in a headache clinic. Using drugs while attending A.A. and N.A. Driving a vehicle while taking drugs. Going to more than one doctor. Going to more than one pharmacy. Going to work on drugs. Overdosing on drugs. Looking for help in a pill. Always counting pills. Mixing medicines. Drinking our daughter and granddaughters codeine cough syrup. Going to church on drugs.

Endangering my family's lives by taking drugs. Being down on my hands and knees looking for one pill I had dropped. My high speed chase when I was drunk as teenager running from the police. Driving a beer truck after drinking. My constant lies to my family. Not spending more time with my precious granddaughters. My new granddaughter had her grandpa driving almost in a coma. Jackie finding me on the floor after my overdose. Dani saying goodbye to me on her way to school for what could have been the last time. Stealing a two dollar bill off of Dani's bulletin board to fill a prescription

The following list of insanities was completed after I returned home. I either forgot about them or purposely omitted them because of fear. Kind of funny now that I look back as I thought some of my insanities were too insane to put down on paper and reveal while I was in treatment. Big mistake, I should have told them everything.

Insanities Continued...

Taking Jackie's pain pills on many occasions and calling her doctor for refills, telling him they were for her. Many times Sasha was my target as I stole her medicine replacing them with another prescription. Breaking into her home and going through cupboards and drawers. Even her daughter's fell victim if their cough syrup had codeine in it. Breaking into Jackie's brother's house to steal his Phenobarbital. Breaking into my oldest daughter's house and stealing Tylox from my son-in-law. The whole Chicago headache clinic story and how I was less than willing. The time I forged a prescription and got caught. My obsessive thoughts of robbing a pharmacy for painkillers. Trying to injure myself so I could get more pills, such as: box cutter to my arm, rock to my arm and leg, cutting my wrist with broken glass, falling down back porch steps on purpose, jumping off the back of a truck to break my leg, heating hot grease to pour on my feet.

All the injections by doctors and nurses and all the lies I told. All the doctors and pharmacies I was seeing at the same time, often in the same day. How I would keep returning to the same ER on the same day until I got what I wanted. My obsessive-compulsive nature. My crazy toothpick and water incident with Stadol. The dragging of my IV stand to steal drugs out of the nurse's station drawer when I was being detoxed. The extreme fear and anxiety I had coming home from work wondering if Jackie would be there or if she had discovered something and left. My tampering with doctors records and shuffling my patient sheets around all in an effort to get painkillers.

Grateful List...

God. My life. Jackie. All of my daughters, grandchildren, mom, dad, brothers, sisters and Jackie's mom and dad. My group in treatment. My health. My job. Dani's counselor at school. Jackie's job. Jackie's visits here in treatment. The fishing trips with Dani. Dani's successful life flight at birth. Dani making the gifted and talented list at school. I'm grateful that I'm alive and have this second chance. That I didn't leave treatment after only a few days. My love for fishing. Hugs from Jackie and Dani. Pictures of my grandchildren. Going several days without a headache.

Page 449 in the Big Book. My oldest daughter going to nursing school. My sponsor. Friends in AA. That I didn't take a life while driving on drugs. Card from my mom. Card from my brother. Handmade gift from Dani. Letter from my sister. That my appetite is back. That my smile is back. That my sense of humor is returning. Nice talk with my mom on the phone. That I have a place to live when I leave. That I have such a wonderful, loving and supportive family. Just feeling better. Feedback from my group. Hugs. Visit from my brother. Compliments from group, family and staff. I am grateful that through prayer God relieved a migraine Sunday and Monday night.

List of Ways I Have Avoided My Feelings...

Isolation. Drugs. Silence. Shutting down. Fishing. Changing jobs. Moving away. Work. Running away. Television. Alcohol. Withdraw. Sleep. Daydreaming. Hiding. Not talking.

What Happens When I Stuff My Feelings...

Headaches. Emotional shutdown. Become distant. Turn to drugs and alcohol. Relationships suffer. Illness. Tend to isolate. Don't make friends. Can't think clearly. No serenity. Lack of intimacy. Listen but don't hear. Cheat your loved ones. Anxiety. Depression. Mind racing. Feeling uneasy. Lack of sleep. Irritable. Lack of concentration. Lose touch with reality. Just don't care anymore. Withdraw. Friendships suffer. People avoid you. Poor outlook on life. Loose contact with God's purpose.

Who Is Mike...

Mike is caring. Mike is dependable. Mike is honest. Mike is a hard worker. Mike chooses his words very carefully. Mike has a fear of failure. Mike has a strong faith in God. Mike is an excellent fisherman. Mike is a good husband and father. Mike is a good grandfather. Mike fears the unknown. Mike had dreams of running in a marathon. Mike is a true friend. Mike is loving. Mike is scared.

Mike is emotional. Mike is sad. Mike is proud. Mike is a perfectionist. Mike believes in family values. Mike over thinks everything. Mike has trouble letting go and letting God. Mike is a people pleaser. Mike can be a blessing to others as he has so been blessed.

What I Like About Mike...

I like that I have strong family values. I like that I am very protective of my family. I like my laugh. I like my smile. I like my insight. I like my ideas. I write good stories. I am patient. I am kind to others. I strive to do the right thing. I like my sense of humor. I take pride in my work. I am a child of God. I am willing to help others. I respect others feelings. I have talent for sports and fishing. I am good with children. I am open to new ideas. I don't follow the crowd. I like that I give hugs. I tell people that I love them. I like that I am faithful to my wife. I like that I am a good father. I like my heart. I like the fact that I want recovery.

What I Get Out Of Being A Perfectionist...

Headaches. Relapses. Poor family relationships. Stress. Anger. Loss of sleep. Conflict with God. No serenity. Tense. Illness. Low self-esteem. Fear of failure. Job burnout. Feelings of being inferior. False pride. Trouble relaxing. I feel good about a job well done. I haven't enjoyed life at its fullest. I can't relax until the work is done. Physical and emotional self-abuse. I believe that I get very little from being a perfectionist.

Another assignment I was given in treatment was to write letters of closure to my dad and Kent, the young man who died before I could get to him. My first letter to dad read:

> 'I was at your bedside when you took your last breath. I was holding your hand. I still am sad almost five years later when I think about it. You were a sports star in high school; young, strong, dark and handsome. Then for reasons unknown to me alcohol came into your life and brought you to your knees, destroying your marriage to mom. Along with cigarettes, the alcohol put you in an early grave. I'm sure you would still be here today but the smoking and alcohol ruined your insides. I'm glad for our relationship through the years and the many talks we had. I want you to know that I'm in treatment for my addictions and that it stops here. I do wish we could have spent more time together when I was a kid. I'm getting treatment so I can spend more time with my ten year old. You

remember your great-granddaughter Danielle. I love you Dad. Your son, Mike.'

Dear Dad letter #2: 'I wanted to let you know how I feel about something you said when I was very young. Dad, during a time when you were drinking quite heavily and your relationship with mom was suffering. You said something to me that I've never forgotten. I remember you putting me on your knee and asking me how I would feel if you had to live somewhere else. Just the fact that I can remember this after all these years tells me it hurt then and I'm carrying that hurt and pain around today. Dad, it's so unfair to put a child in that position. How did I know what to say? I wanted my dad at home to take me fishing and play catch with me. I was also upset when mom found a Playboy magazine in your dresser drawer. This really confused me. A child shouldn't be exposed to such things. Dad, I'm in treatment now for my own addiction and I've learned that your alcoholism was a disease. These two memories of mine I've now been taught are unmanageables in my life. All of our missed opportunities as father and son due to your alcoholism are unmanageable now. They are not my fault. I forgive you dad. I love you dad. I'm searching for serenity dad. Love, your son, Mike.'

'Dear Kent, This letter is to let you know that I cared a great deal for you during your stay at Forest Ridge. I was supposed to pick you up in Sioux City along with some other students after the holidays. Due to bad weather I was a day late to pick you up. That morning before I left the phone rang with the news that you had died. They said it was an accidental shooting. I felt so bad. If I had only picked you up the day before as scheduled. When I picked up the other students they all wanted to know where you were. Of course I was told not to tell them for now. The next day, telling all the residents was so hard, trying to comfort them and all the time hiding my pain. I still have your picture and funeral notice. The funeral was sad for me. I want you to know Kent; I'm forgiving myself for not picking you up on time as it was out of my control. I'll never forget you. Your counselor, Mike.'

By doing these and other assignments while I was in treatment I was able to clear some wreckage from my past. I was released from the bondage of guilt, shame and remorse.

17

I graduated from this center and was released the day before Thanksgiving. Jackie had rented me a small, modest apartment with the idea that we would live apart for six months or so. So that first night found me moving into my new apartment. I borrowed a bed and furniture from my brother and started getting more and more depressed as the night went along. I also went to my work place to break the ice before returning the Monday after Thanksgiving. I was taking on too much too soon, even trying to explain to everyone where I had been all this time. As the night ended and it was time to leave Jackie and Dani and go to my apartment I felt awfully lonely. As I lay in that strange bed in an even stranger apartment I knew I couldn't do this. So I got out of bed, jumped into my clothes and returned home. I spent the night with Jackie. The next day I was on the phone with my landlord trying to get out of there. He agreed to cut me some slack and I proceeded to move back home. I thank Jackie for welcoming me back.

Our checkbook no longer had my name on it and that bothered me, along with the separation of marriage thing. Both issues were soon resolved. So in a very short time, some would argue too soon, I got everything back that I lost. I returned to work on Monday, still quite weak physically and emotionally. I was scared to death to go back to work. After eleven hours we weren't finished but my supervisor noticed that I was. Thank God she sent me home early.

For a few short weeks everything went painfully well and then the cravings started. It's been said that when we forget about our past mistakes that soon they will be repeated, that true insanity is doing the same things over and over again expecting or hoping for different results. As a friend in recovery once told me, 'You have to play the movie of your past using experiences all the way through to the ugly outcome, not just viewing the parts you enjoyed.' I swear that someday, as I'm walking along, there is going to be a huge explosion and it's going to be my head popping out of my ass!

As often times before, it started at work, fellow employees bringing pain pills to work for legitimate reasons. Darvocet for back pain and Tylenol #3 or Vicodin after dental work. I would see them in an unlocked locker, coat pocket or purse. I noticed how extra happy the person was on that certain night they were taking pain pills. One guy even had an assortment in his lunchbox. How could these people just leave this stuff lying out in the open? Didn't they know I just got out of treatment? Didn't they care? On one certain night my supervisor had a bottle of Codeine pills on her desk all night after having dental work. I kept walking by her desk until I knew the strength and how many were left. She seemed to be feeling mighty good that night for someone in physical pain. At one point she asked me if something was wrong. I told her I just had a headache. She asked me if I wanted one of her pain pills. Are you shitting me? I thought to myself. She knew what I was in treatment for!

"No," I said, kind of in shock, "I can't." As I walked away I so wanted to go back and change my no to a yes. Then I realized that she would most likely only give me one pill. If I couldn't have at least four I didn't want to blow my sobriety. What's wrong with these people? Don't they know I crave this stuff? Needless to say, at this point my sobriety was held in place by a frog hair, and I'll just bet it was a Tuesday or Thursday. You see, on these two days very loud country music was played over the radio. For this recovering alcoholic and drug addict country music is like poison, with only a few exceptions. It seemed like every other tune talked about being down and out on alcohol. My attitude could change in an instant by a certain negative tune. Some rock songs would have the same effect. It wasn't long until I was on the phone again testing the waters. My first phone call was to the same out of town pharmacy where I picked up the pills and got pulled over on the way home; I thought maybe I had a refill and sure enough, I did. When I'm in this state of mind I not only get locked in to wanting them, but I have to get them right now. It so happened that after my successful phone call I had to take Dani to her bowling league for a couple of hours. As I sat there and she finished her first of three games my obsession took over. The fact that those pills of instant relief were waiting for me in that little brown bottle just 25 miles away was too much. The insanity returned as I told ten year old Dani that I had an errand to run, but would return before she finished.

I ran out, jumped in my car and sped away. As I reached the highway it hit me, 'Mike are you nuts? You're gonna blow this?' I realized I could never get back in time; and not only would Dani be scared and worried, but she would call Jackie. 'Isn't this fun." I thought looking at myself in the rearview mirror as I hurried back to the bowling alley. I'm sure my disease smiled and said, 'Welcome back Mike! I've been waiting for your return.' Even then, I got back just as Dani was finishing her last game. What was I thinking? So we went home and I came up with some excuse, like taking a walk around the lake and off I went for those precious pills. I returned wondering if all this, including relapsing, was worth it. Especially for 40 pills, a three day supply at best. God gave me plenty of time to change my mind and make the right choice, but it was Mike's self-will that prevailed. I craved that numbness, I didn't want to feel. I continued going to 12 Step Meetings and recording my days of sobriety on the calendar. Sometimes I made it weeks, even months, before selling out in a weak moment. This was my pattern for quite some time, a truly miserable existence.

18

Finally being fed up with being sick and tired, combined with some spirituality by attending frequent meetings I had reached a milestone. By the grace of God I had made it eighteen months clean and sober. I presented the chip symbolizing my accomplishment to Jackie and Dani as I returned home from the meeting. Although I knew this to be nothing short of a miracle, my inner cords of faith were becoming frayed with fear. My behavior and attitude at work had been slipping for a couple of months now. I was setting myself up for one big thing, a set back, that would snap those cords of faith and hope. I may have been off the pills and alcohol, but I still suffered from all the '-isms' that are part of alcoholism.

My anger and the my-way-or-the-highway attitude at work continued to rob me of peace and serenity. After 18 months it was time to move onto the next level of my sobriety. Little did I realize at the time that this next level required some action on my part. I needed to do much more than just sit back and boast about my clean time. Well, sure enough, that straw broke the camel's back. Reluctant at first, I would make doctors appointments only to cancel them as I regained my senses. It was at work one night, sitting at the break table, that I overheard a conversation that would be instrumental in my selling out after 18 months. A girl I worked with was telling a young man about her recent visit to a new doctor in town. I recalled her telling him that this new doc gave her painkillers and asked her if she needed anything else and told her he had a whole pad of blank prescriptions. I'm sure he was joking with her but his name was now etched in my mind and when those cords of hope snapped, which they soon did, I would pay him a visit.

19

Often times the lower-power of addiction sends a lone sniper to derail our recovery. In May of 2001 however, 'the creep from the deep,' as a friend in recovery calls him, sent a whole battalion after me. I forgot during this onslaught that this lower power of addiction is not equal or above the power of the Almighty God; Father, Son and Holy Spirit. This devil was defeated long ago. Victory has been won for us on the cross by Jesus. This creep from the deep will win some battles along the way, but the war is over. Victory is ours in the struggle, if we would just claim it. As the Bible verse says, "No temptation is so great that God would not always provide a way out along with the temptation." The choice ultimately is ours as it comes back to that free will thing. I believe we should let God's will run its course, or else our free will may change our course. When I forget God's will I'm soon back to a state of powerlessness.

So what could possibly get in the way of 18 months of clean time? Little stuff, lots and lots of little stuff! I relapsed on May 31st, always a dangerous month for me. Here's the list of May Madness that drove me back to my best friend and worst enemy. First of all I should share with you about the May curse I've had since my teen years. For some reason my AK-47 side rears its ugly head in May. I've thought about this for years, trying to figure out what it is about the month of May. Here's what I've come up with…

May is officially the end of winter hibernation. The sounds of birds, lawnmowers and motorcycles have broken the silence of winter. Closed windows are now open to the smell of outdoor grilling and children playing outside, sometimes very loudly. My passion for fishing kicks in with anxiety attached. So much fishing to do and so little time. What if they're biting and I have to go back to work? Maybe this year I won't go at all, yeah right? Area softball games and other outdoor activities associated with festive socializing and of course alcohol. Beer gardens, radio and TV ads make that cold beer look so inviting. Did you know the Coors Light label now turns blue in your refrigerator when its ice cold and time to drink? Too much information for me! Pets and wildlife act weird in May. Could this explain my restlessness? I know I'm reaching on this one. "If it feels good do it," and "Eat, drink and be merry for tomorrow we die," replaces thoughts like, "Let go and let God."

If the Garth Brooks song, "I've got friends in low places," comes on the radio I'm off and running nowhere again. I've listed five reasons, or maybe five excuses, why May has been my downfall. After my May 31st relapse I would write in my journal, 'Fell one day short of getting through the terrible month of May.' Let's get back to the madness of 2001 and why I sold out one day short of celebrating victory over May. Work woes would certainly top the list. This was one of our busiest months of the year meaning long hours and short fuses. Break time was especially frustrating as employees discussed their weekend plans. Campouts, graduation parties, Memorial Day weekend or just plans to hit the bar on 'Thirsty Thursday' after a long week. I made a habit not to bring extra money to work, just enough for a milk and a soda. This saved my butt many a time at the end of a long work day when it's 'Miller Time.' I had just taken a week's vacation in late April to rest up for the wrath of May. I went fishing and the way I fish isn't always relaxing to say the least. A journal entry during this time off reads like this: 'Vacation 2001, 250 crappies and 20 jumbo perch in four days fishing at Herm's Pond. 4/26, 4/27, 4/28 and 4/30.'

I should mention also that it's about a quarter of a mile walk to this pond through hills, pastures and over electric fences. So much for a little down time before heading back to work. I love to fish more than anything, but I fish in excess because of the euphoria I get. At 48 years old I wasn't exactly a well conditioned athlete either.

May fourth was my two year anniversary of my near fatal overdose. I'm sure many mixed emotions accompanied this. May fifth I received my 18 month chip for alcoholic abstinence, but in all honesty it had only been 13 or 14 months since my last pill or injection. Being the perfectionist I was I'm sure my fudging on a couple of months bothered me also. The first Friday of each month I traveled to a nearby treatment center to tell my personal story of addiction. Often times listening to other addicts afterward. Sharing their knowledge of pharmaceuticals would set me up for cravings on the drive home. May 14 was Mother's Day which meant a visit with my mom, and for some reason we discussed her prized coin collection that I stole from her as teenager for gas money to run a way from home. On May 15 a young man that I had worked with and visited with in recovery hung himself at home and was discovered by his 12 year old daughter. Tim was only 37 years old and suffered from migraines also. Alcohol stripped him of any hope for himself. I felt the pain of missed opportunities to maybe have helped him in someway. May 18 was my first visit to my sister and brother-in-law's since their intervention in 1999. Roger wasn't only married to my sister, but was also my best friend for many years. He had just returned home from cancer surgery. We sat and visited a little bit about him and too much about my recovery. Somehow, out of nowhere, that coin collection incident came up for the second time that week. I drove home on a wing and prayer as those cords of faith and hope had weakened.

May 22 was the night I overhead the conversation at work. This is what I recorded in my journal: 'Probably my worst night at work since going drug free! All of my character defects and shortcomings were exposed.' 'Came oh, so close to a relapse after overhearing conversation between L and B about how easy Dr. M and Dr. K are. They give you whatever you want.' I most certainly am a drug addict. May 24 was my big blow-up at work. You see, I have a pattern, a defect of character that causes me to stuff my feelings. If you've ever overloaded a washing machine you know what I mean. After stuffing it full you find a couple of dirty towels and stuff them in. Then it spins out of control, it shakes and rattles and it seems to holler, 'I'm full! I can't handle all this dirty laundry!' If some of that dirty laundry isn't removed it finally shuts down. My May 25 journal entry reads, 'I finally blew-up at work last night and feel like total shit today. Followed by acceptance, until I can grasp on to this simple concept I shall never know peace. I'M HURTING!' The evening of May 25 found me traveling to an out of town meeting with my temporary sponsor. I ranted and raved all the way there about how we and the other 12-steppers had failed to help Tim before he took his own life. I'm sure I went over the top resulting in the 'The Letter' I would receive from him in a few days.

May 25 through the 27; the self-inflicted stress associated with these days alone pushed me over the edge for an hour or so. You see, Dani was not only born on May 27th, 12 years ago but Jackie and I were married on this day some 29 years earlier. Yes, God sent Dani to us on our anniversary. Combined with the other happenings of the month I was on an emotional roller coaster. That using mechanism kicked in, telling me I couldn't get through this special day and Memorial weekend without some chemical help. So during this hour of poor me's I focused only on instant relief. I called Dr. M's clinic and made an appointment. The nurse told me to come right in since they had an opening in about 15 minutes. As I scurried around the house looking for the box of blank checks, I felt the old behavior returning. I located the checks way to easy. I realized it was because Jackie felt she didn't have to hide them anymore. She trusted me- ouch! This ruined the moment. As I tore out two blank checks I noticed that my name was back on the checks instead of just hers. My pre-drug high was getting a serious reality check. The last thing to do was to get my insurance card out of my wallet. As I sorted through the cards I ran across a piece of paper I wrote a note on some time ago. It was a line from LeAnn Womack's new single, "I Hope You Dance.' The line jumped out at me as I read it, "When you come close to selling out, reconsider." I told myself I didn't want to do this. I was back in reality knowing I was about to throw 18 months out the window. I called the doctors office back, canceling my appointment. I went back into our bedroom hitting my knees and thanking God for sparing me this moment of emotional crisis.

May 28 was the Tuesday after Memorial Day and I thought I had made it, that is, until there was a knock on the door. It was the private contractor Jackie had hired to replace our front living room window with a huge bay window. This meant that a large chunk of our wall was about to be knocked out. He took one step into our living room and said that all the stuff was going to have to be moved away from the wall. All I could think was that I had to work that night and I needed a nap. As he returned to his truck I started to rearrange the living room. I stopped in my tracks when I saw our two movie towers standing in front of the wall. I'm talking hundreds of movies that I would have to box up. I finished up in time to grab a couple hours of sleep before work. Have you ever tried to nap when someone is tearing a hole in your wall? I went to work in a condition treatment centers call H.A.L.T. which means to stop and take a self-inventory. Am I hungry, angry, lonely or tired? I may not have been hungry or lonely, but I was extremely tired and as angry as a Pit Bull with an abscessed tooth. So basically I was all set for a peaceful night at work, that is, as long as nobody looked at me, spoke to me or stood too close to me.

May 30 arrived and found me sleeping in the basement after a long night at work. I couldn't hide from the noise and what if he asked me what goes where? I wandered up the stairs and to this day I still don't know why, but I checked the mailbox. In recovery I usually avoided the mail as it was just another trigger for my stress. I gathered up the few envelopes and stumbled into the kitchen as I was still exhausted. On top was a letter addressed to me from my temporary sponsor. 'Thank you Lord,'

I thought as I opened it. Surely it was a letter of encouragement as he knew I was knee deep in emotional baggage after what I shared with him the other night. I couldn't have been more wrong.

I read the letter in disbelief sinking lower and lower into my chair. Again and again I read lines like, 'How selfish of you to think that yours is the only message that should be told at treatment centers,' and, 'I know this will cause problems for you. Problems in addiction and problems in life.' 'You need to get more active in service work... I know it's boring.' 'It needs to be done by people who GIVE-A-SHIT about people struggling in recovery.' 'It's time to admit you care. It's time you started doing something about it.' He signed it, 'Yours in service.'

My counselor once told me that there are no big shots in recovery, but by the grace of God only humble servants. I've always responded better to criticism with kid gloves. This letter instead was a right hook from Mike Tyson. How dare he imply that I don't care? I do care! Maybe too much, and not one mention of Tim, the struggling alcoholic who just two weeks earlier had hung himself in despair. I didn't go to work that night. Jackie read the letter and consoled me the best she could. I was emotionally and physically drained. I just went to bed and escaped through sleep. First, though, I called him in tears and asked for an explanation, but the comfort I was seeking wasn't there.

I awoke the morning of Friday, May 31st tired, confused and still clinging to that resentment. I made it until early afternoon, pulling the letter out of the envelope and rereading it. I called into work sick for a second night and my plan to escape unfolded. I would go see Dr. M and work him for every narcotic pain pill I could. After all, who could blame me in this state of depression? It was either relapse or start planning for my own funeral. I convinced myself that even my family would support me on this one. I felt no guilt as I made the doctor appointment. I was totally justified this time. Of course I knew I was lying to myself and that God could and would have helped me. In a strange way God used that relapse to bring me closer to him. For this reason I know I can thank that sponsor for the letter and the good that eventually came from it.

20

I wasn't disappointed in Dr. M as he didn't question my actions that day and never inquired about my medical or patient history. He has long since left this area along with many other doctors who, for a time, were known for their 'generosity' when it came to narcotics. To my best memory I was given 60 Ultram and 60 Vicoprofen that afternoon. Not bad for my first visit. He told me I could call in for more refills. Wow! How cool was that? At the time I truly believed I was doing the 'the next right thing,' because the 'right thing,' in my twisted thinking, was to take all 120 of these and lay down for a dirt nap. After all, who would care? They didn't care about Tim so why would they care about me? On my way to the pharmacy I was already feeling that pre-drug high as I clutched the prescriptions in my hand. My initial thought was to take them as prescribed by the doctor. After all, it's been 18 months; one of each should do the trick. As I returned to my car with the two bottles of pills hidden in my pocket I was already rethinking the dosage, two of each, but that was it. Reality struck 24 hours later when I realized I had taken 12 of these painkillers in one day. My hunger for numbness and tolerance for narcotics hadn't weakened in a year and a half. I do believe what they say in recovery, this disease continues to grow even when we're abstaining from drugs and alcohol. We quickly return to where we left off and then even more to cover all the guilt.

The next two weeks would see two family outings marred by my return to narcotics. June second was the Kid's Fishing Derby at the lake. Dani was in the senior division this year after taking first place three out of the last four years. She had always out fished the boys in her group and with me pre-fishing the week before for the hot spot it was no wonder she would catch 30 to 40 fish in four hours. I frantically took the fish off, baited her hook and told her to get back out there! If I hadn't been so hyped up on all those pills it would have been the relaxing father and daughter moment it was meant to be. On that day Dani would take top honors again doubling or tripling the total fish of the boy competitors. Dani hasn't fished with me for many years and who could blame her? She just got burned out.

I took a few days off work and the three of us made a trip to Dyersville to visit where the movie, *The Field of Dreams* was filmed. This was my idea after watching the movie the first night after scoring on all those pills. This was old behavior and quite common for me when I'm feeling that good while under the influence. Big ideas at the spur of the moment. Decisions made when I was high rarely worked out. So off we went with plans to get a motel room for the night and visit the Amana Colonies the next day. I had my pills in my pocket and was ready for a road trip. Upon arriving at the motel to check in before spending the day at The Field of Dreams reality hit. I picked a fight with Jackie over something trivial as Dani stood close by. I wanted everything to be perfect and I was already blowing it. So I was off to the bathroom for a handful of pills and then all would be better. After just a few days of relapsing I was drowning again.

We arrived at the ballpark, set in the middle of a cornfield, and it was really quite spectacular. Everything looked just as it did in the movie, except for the concession stand and the souvenir shop. Some children were playing a game of baseball on the infield as we walked towards the outfield surrounded by corn. 'Is this heaven?' I thought, 'No, it's Iowa and you're high again.' I quickly did something I only do when I'm in that false state of well being. I spotted a baseball lying in the grass, 'I gotta have this!' A baseball from The Field of Dreams, what a prized possession. I didn't give a thought to the fact that I was stealing in front of my daughter. Off to the car I went to tuck it away. I seldom, if ever, act like this when I'm clean and sober. It's different when I'm using because I think the rules don't apply and I get itchy fingers. That night as Jackie and Dani slept in the motel I sat in front of the TV, bug eyed and popping pills. With the baseball in hand I carefully inked it with all the details that would make it a memory of our trip. Sadly all that I really remember of this family outing was that the pills robbed me of truly enjoying time spent with Jackie and Dani.

May 31st quickly became August 31st and I was back in treatment under a court committal again. After nearly 18 months of clean time I had sought out and swallowed approximately 1,300 narcotic pain pills, many injections and alcohol whenever necessary. As the county sheriff pulled into our driveway I headed for the bedroom taking the last 20 tranquilizers I had left. This, mixed with the pain pills I took hours earlier, took their effect as we arrived at the treatment facility. I couldn't even standup so they brought a wheelchair to the sheriff's car.

I don't remember much after that except for the two female patients who wheeled me outside so I could have a couple of smokes; and the next morning in the day room. I'll never forget that pain and shame. You see, it wasn't only Friday, but it was my Friday. Once a month I traveled here to tell my story of how I managed to stay clean and sober for a year and a half. I treasured this hour once a month offering hope to hopeless addicts and alcoholics. The last time I spoke here was in May, just days after my relapse. I talked the talk, but God knew I wasn't walking the walk anymore. My June and July lectures didn't happen, I cancelled out on both of these, claiming I was sick or some other excuse. So there I sat as someone approached the bulletin board to see who would be their speaker that morning. The lecturer who was scheduled for that day was Mike D.

"Anybody know who Mike D. is?" they asked.

"Yeah," I responded, "I used to." I explained that it was me but there would be no lecture that morning. I had just hit another bottom as I sat there humbled, broken and still foggy from all the pills the afternoon before. It would be some 13 months until this treatment center put me back on their lecture schedule. I proceeded to screw it up again when I had my hernia surgery. Oh yes, some pain medication they would have understood, but the only time I've ever said no to pain pills is when I misunderstood the question! If I'd asked for help and stuck to it I wouldn't have lost anything except for the hernias. The only plan I had was to get high and stay high as long as I could by milking the doctors out of narcotics. To this day I haven't re-applied to be a speaker. A pill here or an injection there has always tainted my honesty. "Fall down seven times but get up eight," became my favorite motto.

After three days of detoxing I made my court appearance. This time the judge was a bit more lenient. All of the state funded facilities were already filled up with recovering drug addicts and alcoholics. So, by the grace of God, I got a break. My court transcript read as follows:

"In the matter of Michael G. Dryden alleged to be a substance abuser. The court is in receipt of the physicians report indicating that the respondent is a chronic substance abuser. Said report recommends inpatient treatment. However, no state funded facilities are available. Only Manning hospital is available and respondent is unable to afford same. Both the attorney for respondent and the applicant consent to an alternative outpatient situation. The court believes that the additional debt of $6,200 resulting from inpatient care would cause unfounded additional stress on respondent. Further, respondent should be given the opportunity to resolve his problems on an outpatient basis. The undersigned finds that the contention that the respondent is a substance abuser has been sustained by clear and convincing evidence based both on the report and the respondents own consent. Therefore, it is hereby ordered that the respondent is directed to outpatient treatment at New View in Carroll. Respondent shall report to New View daily to verify that he has not again started abusing substances. He shall also report only to Dr. P for medical treatment except for true emergencies. It is further ordered that the administrator of the above noted facility shall report to the undersigned as required by law noting his progress."

So Jackie and Dani, reluctant but always supportive, drove me back to our home. I knew once again that this was my last chance; that all my rescues and get out of jail free cards were used up. As we returned home I was accompanied by three constant companions; guilt, shame and remorse. The Dani factor always cut the deepest and hurt the most. I knew I would never forget the sheriff's car in our driveway. She was next door that day, probably watching the whole ordeal out the window. I'm sure she suffered her own shame that day as her best friend lived right across the street and her dad is a Deputy Sheriff.

This would be my last true intervention as my recovery continued with a few slips along the way. My survival was based on three things: God, meetings and service. After each slip God picked me up and dusted me off only to see me fall again, but something spiritual was happening along the way. I was gaining some confidence, hope and faith. I felt a calling in service to others, a purpose, and strength out of my own personal weakness.

21

Now I'd like to share with you my personal recovery roller coaster based on the solid foundation of spirituality. When I interject humor along the way please understand that this helps me deal with life on life's terms. It isn't meant to downplay the seriousness of this disease in any way.

Let's start with the bubble test they give you in treatment. I believe I did a total of three of these. They all came back stating that I had a serious case of depression. If you've ever taken one of these multi-page question and answer tests you probably got depressed along the way too. It usually took me up to three days just to complete one. Some of the questions were simple, no-brainers, others seemed tricky and some were just downright weird. Here are some 'slightly exaggerated' examples of the questions asked in the infamous treatment bubble test.

If three is blue and six is red what color is nine? If a tree falls in the forest and no one is around to hear it, what kind of tree is it? I don't know! Maybe a Dutch Elm? Have you ever brushed your teeth with Preparation H and put Crest up your butt? If a glass is full and not empty, what's in the glass?

If it's 1:00 PM in Chicago and 10:00 AM in Sydney, Australia, what color is the sky in Montana? If March comes in like a lion and goes out like a lamb, how many addicts will relapse on April Fool's Day? Would you be willing to be a test dummy in a guillotine factory? If Joe is ten and Julie is seven, what did Ralph have for breakfast? I'm pretty sure it wasn't scrambled eggs with chunks of fish!

What does a meth addict have to look forward to on Easter? Who knows maybe The Ether Bunny!

I'll tell you one thing, just the fear of taking another one of these tests is enough to keep a person clean and sober. So I was back at home and detoxing as Jackie was given 12 pills to finish my tapering off. Believe me, finding a needle in a haystack would have been easier than locating where Jackie had those hidden. She was quite stingy too, the last few doses she even cut in half!

The date of the second day of being totally drug free is one I'll never forget and will remain in history forever. September 11, 2001 found me in the bathroom shaving nervously as I turned on the radio at about 8:30 AM to my favorite light music station. I'm sure I was wishing I had half a pill left. Ten or 15 minutes later the music was interrupted by news that none of us will ever forget. There was a 12 Step meeting downtown at 10:00. My second day of sobriety was being tested and I was severely at risk.

I finished getting ready and hurried to my meeting as the radio said that we were under attack. I'll never forget the meeting that morning as recovering addicts and alcoholics offered an extra measure of support to one another. The main theme was that we didn't have to drink or do drugs over this situation. God put us all together that morning in the only safe haven we knew. We were surrounded by local bars and pharmacies. I don't think any of us wanted to leave the meeting that day. Returning to our radios and TV sets would be a far cry from the fellowship we just enjoyed.

I was supposed to return to work that night but getting in a nap wasn't my main concern. I went next door to Sasha's house and we tried consoling each other. She asked me if I was going to be ok and I told her that I went to a meeting, avoiding the fact that I wasn't ok. About then her phone rang; it was my oldest daughter calling from her home some distance away. Janna is Dani's biological mom and hadn't spoken to us in quiet some time.

As I listened I surely thought that because of this terrorist situation she would want to talk to me. There would be no father-daughter reunion today as Sasha hung up the phone.

"She didn't ask to speak to me?" I asked Sasha.

"No dad. She just was angry and said she didn't want to be part of this family anymore." Wow! That was quite a dagger in my heart, especially on a day when none of us knew what would lie ahead for our country or our families. It should have been a day for us to reunite, not to separate over petty differences. My first thought was relapse, but I figured that every doctor in town would have a red flag out for me if I appeared on their doorstep, especially on this tragic day. Besides, there was that court order saying that I only see our family doctor, sponsor and long time friend. He surely would have offered some comfort but definitely no narcotics! So off to work I went where the comfort of true fellowship was replaced by employees frantically running to the gas station at break time because of rumors that gasoline would soon reach $5.00 a gallon.

I did put together another 18 months or, by my calculations, about two years of sobriety. God, meetings and service were always my foundation. I did pretty well away from work, but work was like a war zone. The spirituality associated with recovery was hard to find in the workplace, especially in our hometown, which boasts of its Catholic heritage on the surface. My eyes and ears picked up on a different heritage, that of "If it feels good do it," and "Eat, drink and be merry for tomorrow we die," Sadly, many have died right here in our midst. Too many young people have been lost, following the footsteps of misguided parents. Break time at work took a toll on any serenity I obtained by trying to do the right thing. Gossip, character assassination, inappropriate sex talk, tasteless jokes and alcohol have had an ugly grip on this town since I was a child.

So after another stretch of sobriety those cords of faith started to fray again. It was April of 2004 with that dreaded month just around the corner. I had taken some vacation time to unwind before the attack of the May demons. I don't think that 'been there, done that,' ever occurred to me. Morning, noon and night found me chasing fish. One night, around 10:00, I stopped in Wal-Mart for some last minute jig heads before driving two hours north for a night of walleye fishing. There, standing in the fishing section, was a friend in recovery. Ron and I had known each other since we were kids. We had something in common besides a passion for fishing though. Ron, like me, had his own history of prescription drug and alcohol abuse. He asked me if I was going fishing and I told him that I was. When I told him I was headed to Lost Island he asked me if I wanted some company. I told him that would be great but that I would probably be there all night and half of the day tomorrow. I think I was hoping that he would pass as I'm definitely a lone wolf when fishing, but Ron was as hardcore as I was when it came to fishing, so we went to his house for some gear. It turned out he was probably the only person with more tackle than me. My Topaz looked more like we were going for two weeks after he added his stuff. One thing I've noticed over the years is that recovering alcoholics and addicts sure have similar personality traits. Moderation in anything is so hard for us, excess is our rule. The two of us together were lethal in the excess field. Those poor fish aren't going to know what hit them!

After some 19 hours we returned home. Three lakes and a river later my cooler was full of fish. As we drove home Ron even calculated how many fish an hour we would have to had caught to make the trip a success. We were two peas in a pod, both headed for a relapse and neither one knew the other was going to sell out. Ron confided in me some time later that he was under the influence of pills that night. I suspected that he was as he seemed to be feeling pretty good, if you know what I mean. As I was hurting and struggling with those constant cravings he seemed to be experiencing no pain which made me very suspicious. Once again, as they say in recovery, 'You can fool the fans, but you can't fool the players.'

The month of May arrived as it always had. My disease had been patiently waiting for me. While I was fishing and sleeping it was working out, getting stronger and stronger. This monster called addiction feeds on problems at work, emotional turmoil, doubts, worries and fear. One Sunday afternoon in May found me driving home from a very successful fishing trip. I had a mess of fished iced down in the cooler including the one that would get my Big Fish Award for the year. Just a block from home I stopped at a neighborhood convenience store for a Mountain Dew. That euphoria that I get from fishing was running through my veins. With little regard for my clean time I grabbed three 24 ounce cans of beer as the soda just wouldn't 'dew it' any longer.

My addiction wins again, Mike's a loser and life on life's terms sucks. So I went back to my best friend/worst enemy who promised the numbness that I craved. I'd worry about death and destruction later. It was Sunday and I had to go to that job I hate tomorrow. I was going to clean fish, drown out the pain and celebrate my fishing success. A few ice cold beers later I was off and running to make the summer of 2004 one I'd never forget. My theme for that summer was the Nickleback hit that went, "... something's gotta go wrong because I'm feelin' way to damn good." I was feeling good as I socialized with fellow employees, joining in on all the negative gossip and the poor attitudes that drove me crazy while I was trying to take the path to recovery. I was one of them now; a loose cannon, a free spirit, not answering to anyone. The problem was the fact that I knew there was a God and I was called to work for him, not against him. I quit going to meetings and church as I didn't want to be reminded that there was something better out there. I'll be miserable but at least I'll be having fun!

The so-called fun continued to elude me as my alcohol consumption increased. You see, the summer of my coming out party I decided that I would just drink alcohol and stay away from the pills. It's so baffling how we can lie to ourselves and believe the lie. "After all," I thought, "the narcotics are what always bring you to your knees, alcohol you can handle, and look at the plus side, no doctors, no pharmacies, no prescriptions and no high priced pills compared to beer. Most every place in town carries this socially acceptable painkiller called alcohol." What was I thinking, all those years chasing narcotics.

Yes, alcohol is definitely the answer to my pain and I thought that I could control alcohol and not have it control me like those wicked pills did. I still don't know what color the sky was in my world that summer. By late July things were going wrong again and I wasn't feeling good at all. I believed the lie and, in fishing terms, took the bait hook, line and sinker.

What started as an occasional six pack after work became an obsession. I quickly discovered, during my brief social life that summer that I didn't drink like other people. After an all nighter I was ready to do it again the next day. Those fair weather drinking friends were nowhere to be found so I drank alone. Weekends found me passing out twice as I could start popping the tops at the crack of dawn and upon awakening later that afternoon I couldn't face the emotional pain so I drank until bedtime. Most of the time I hid this from Dani and Jackie but they knew that I was drinking again. I would purchase the beer and ice on the way to work so I could drink the minute I reached the car.

22

Two or three months later the alcohol just wouldn't do it anymore. I couldn't even get through a day without obsessing about pharmaceuticals. Sure, I could put vodka or Everclear in my water bottle at work but those pills started calling me again. After all, people would notice me getting drunk at work. Pills, on the other hand, just enhanced my performance. No hangovers, no pain and no alcohol smell. Yes, pills would be the answer to my problems today—not! My butt was kicked in just weeks this time as I still drank and swallowed the few pills I was able to score on. I got so sick, so fast I spent a week on the sofa unable to work. I got my past recovery material out and started reading again. I ran across old painful articles of support from family and friends while I had been clean and sober. These were cards and notes that slapped me in the face that summer of fun in 2004. The big blow was when I read things Dani had written to me along my path of recovery. She usually gave me these special notes when she could see that I was struggling to keep my addicted head above water. Here are some of those special notes from Dani.

"Dad, I found a quote for you—'Recovery is a process not an event." "Dad, Carla called to congratulate you on your one year." "Dad, you shouldn't worry so much."

Along with many special hand made cards and one very special Father's Day card that has gotten me through another 24 hours many times. 'Happy Father's Day,' she colored on the front along with a fish, a pole and a can of bait. Inside she drew and colored a huge bobber. In a child's hand writing she wrote the following:

Top Ten Reasons You're My Dad

You're loving. You care. You take me fishing. You come to my softball games. You practice softball with me. You are nice. You go to church with me. You say the prayers at supper. You always listen when I talk to you. Just because you're my dad!

Happy Father's Day

Love Dani

Thank you Dani for all your love, support and understanding. Thank God for putting you in my life. I received many notes, cards and letters from Sasha also. One such letter on my fiftieth birthday reads:

"Happy Birthday Dad" Wow, fifty years old. I can't believe that. Even though the numbers keep going up you don't seem to age. To me you're still the same fun loving dad you were when I was little, but one thing you have gotten through the years is wiser and stronger (and maybe a little smarter too). This is an important month for you. Not just for your birthday but also in your journey of going through life drug free. I am so very proud of you and if I end up with just half of your courage and strength and faith I will be a very lucky person. I wish you the best of luck in work, recovery and most of all fishing (with me) in the next year. I love you dad. Sasha.

I love you also Sasha, more than words can say. I hope and pray that you find the same peace I've been searching for my entire life. To my first born and oldest daughter, Janna. Even though distance and conflicts have separated us, you always will hold a special place in my heart. I know you also never gave up on me and would fight for me to the bitter end. Thanks for the road trip with me to Cherokee for a very special two hour meeting. Please pray for me and I'll pray for you. Then there's my wife, best friend and spiritual advisor, Jackie. Even though the depth of my constant cravings for mood altering chemicals is foreign to her, she showers me with compassion, love, support and prayers. Countless handmade notes, cards and flyers would show up during my toughest of times in my lunchbox at work, on my desk at home and post-it notes around the house. Jackie, truly you are the wind beneath this addicts wings and without it I'm a lost soul. You are without a doubt a gift from God and the unconditional love you have given me I can never repay. Thank you, most of all. You give me hope, purpose and direction. I now understand why husbands often refer to their wives as their other half because without you I could never be whole.

In August of 2004, with all of this support and love, I pulled myself off the sofa and went back to work. I even tried changing shifts, going from nights to days to mid-shift and back to days again. I found that with each shift change not only came headaches but a variety of stress. Despite my best efforts to stay off the painkillers I continued to sell out in moments of emotional turmoil. I have kept the alcohol from touching my lips but those darn pharmacies are so cunning, baffling, powerful and patient. The saying is true for us in recovery that, 'Seven days without a meeting makes one weak.' Every time, and I do mean every time, I've strayed from God, meetings and service I end up with pills in my pocket. I truly believe what 12 step meetings have taught me that God could and would help us if we would just ask him. I remember one painful trip to work when I was fighting that urge to take a detour to the doctor's office.

I was hurting so bad as I passed a familiar church, still debating what my choice would be. As I looked up on the roof of that church I passed almost everyday, something caught my eye. Even though my car wanted to turn off my path and seek pain relief I saw the cross, and with tears running down my face I said the most powerful prayer that I can remember. For a moment I got out of my head and into my heart. I looked at the cross and said my one word prayer, HELP! That was it. Just then my favorite song by Sarah McLaughlin came on the radio, telling me that I was, "... in the arms of an angel..." When I arrived at work there were only two people sitting outside the door. Out of several hundred employees these two just happened to be in recovery also. Coincidence? I think not!

Since then I seldom, if ever, forget to look upon that cross as I pass by. I continued to put weeks and months of clean time together. At meetings I would often boast of my H.O.P.E. formula. Hold On Pray Everyday. I would write notes like, 'our disease preys on us everyday so we need to pray everyday.' I would purchase almost anything that had the word hope on it, but when that 'creep from the deep' came calling I would quickly lose hope and quit praying. That lower power of addiction seemed to always know when to strike. Finding me tired and angry at work it would prey on me there. For a couple more years I would go to the phone at work in random moments of crisis calling a variety of doctors in and out of town. If I would score on some pills I would leave work to go get them. I had to have them now! Just knowing they were waiting for me at the pharmacy wasn't enough.

The insanity of my merry-go-round of personality clashes still continued. It was that old behavior of minister versus AK-47, always the two extremes. Please understand that I did have lengthy periods of peace, joy and serenity. This was the byproduct of doing the right thing as I believe God guided me, but when the attack came I was often swept away by the attraction of not feeling.

One such time I picked up a prescription for 60 painkillers after a bad day. I brought them to work as I always did and secured them in my locker with a padlock. Near the days end I was in the restroom, popping a handful of pills to insure a mellow evening. I looked at the bottle and noticed the pill count seemed low. I hurried home, closed the bedroom door and poured them out on the bed. Frantically I counted as there didn't seem to be the right amount of pills. Sure enough the bottle said 60 but when I added the amount I took that day with what was left in the bottle I came up 20 short. Somebody alert the D.E.A, I've been ripped off! My first thought was my locker at work, but it wasn't only locked I also had the bottle wrapped in a handkerchief for extra protection. No one was going to help themselves to this addicts supply! Suddenly it struck me that it must have been the pharmacist. Yeah, that's it; he only gave me 40 instead of 60. Then I had a moment of reality. I was being shown the craziness of my actions. I would just let go and let God back into my life. After all, I still had 20 pills to get through the next couple of days. That plan lasted about 24 hours as the next day I was on the phone to that pharmacy. 'He won't believe me,' I thought as I listened to the phone ring. They know I'm a pill junkie and will just think I'm conning them out of twenty more pills. The gentleman answered and I told him what must have happened. His normally pleasant tone turned to anger as he stood his ground that I was given all 60, not 40. He stated that I must have been mistaken or been the victim of somebody at work. Humbly I agreed and hung up the phone. I did have a few pills left so I would take them all and forget about it. Once again 'true insanity is doing the same thing over and over and expecting different results.'

As the next day arrived I found myself not only out of pills but obsessing over the fact that I was right and he was wrong. My sickness surfaced with vengeance. I harassed this poor pharmacist over and over till he gave in. I finally had my 20 pills. Realizing just how pathetic my actions were, I pledged to taper myself off with these 20 precious pills and then quit this madness forever. I must clearly state that God wasn't letting me down. It was only by his grace and mercy that I survived to tell of this miracle in my life. Dead men do tell tales when God's message needs to be heard. I believe this with every fiber of my being. I noticed toward the end of my spontaneous sell-outs that this God of hope was intervening. I have written many letters over the years to a variety of doctors and pharmacies to expose myself. This has spared me countless relapses, but it is ultimately up to us to completely surrender and let go and let God. Addiction and alcoholism makes for a very dark life but God does his best work in the dark. We just need to seek him, if only half as much as we sought the drugs and alcohol.

My hope and reason for writing this book is so all those suffering may find this God of miracles. My final few encounters with relapses were pointless and accomplished nothing but heartache. One Saturday found me home alone and emotionally vulnerable. In moments like these I would often call the pharmacies to see if I had any refills. I knew I didn't but the phone call gave me a twisted rush of sorts. I made a call to one of many of these and to my shock I scored. A new pharmacist that didn't know me said I didn't have any refills but maybe she could help. This actually scared me because in my heart I was hoping she would turn me down. She offered to give me ten painkillers so I could make it through the weekend. She said that she would just fax a request for a refill to the doctor's office on Monday and tell them that I already received 10 pills on Saturday. They didn't even charge me for these I thought as I swallowed all 10 before leaving the parking lot.

By this stage of my using, a great deal of guilt accompanied a relapse. I knew I was going against God's will for me. I also knew I was playing Russian Roulette with each prescription. Would these 10 pills lead me to the abyss once again? Or is my self will going to lead me to jail, an institution or the morgue? It then occurred to me that the doctor's office on Monday would see what I did when they receive the fax. I had just written them a letter weeks earlier telling them of my addiction. I sure knew how to ruin a high I realized as I tried to relax. I would just deal with this on Monday. Well, Monday came as it always does and I was at work having an anxiety attack over what actions the doctor would take after receiving the fax sent on Saturday. At our 11:00 AM lunch break I couldn't stand it anymore. I knew I had to go to the doctor's office for a little damage control. That using voice told me that maybe they never got my letter and if not, there just may be a refill waiting for me. So off I went, having only half an hour to fix this mess and maybe score on some more pills. As I approached the nurse's station I didn't have a chance to say anything before the nurse said, "Hi Mike. We received a refill request from the pharmacy. We figured it must be a mistake as your letter to us stated that you are court ordered to see Dr. P. only."

She was quite polite to me as I think they were relieved to get my letter and to not have to deal with a problem patient anymore. I thanked her which was pretty much lip service only as I had an even bigger problem. The nurse told me they had faxed this whole mess over to Dr. P's office. This wasn't good as Dr. P was my sponsor and had saved my life after my overdose. He also agreed with my family to have me court committed… twice. I could be knee deep in trouble over this thing. Still on my 30-minute lunch break I hurried back to Dr. P's office. Nervously I questioned the receptionist to see if they had received a refill request for me. She couldn't find it and Dr. P was with a patient. I told her to just ignore it when it came in as it was all just a mistake. Yeah, my mistake, not trusting in God again. At this point in my on again off again recovery I was becoming desperate. God, meetings and service were my refuge. I knew the rewards of helping others and expecting nothing in return. I tested God with this many times, and have come to believe this simple truth. In serving others with no personal motive for yourself, except to stay clean and sober, the rewards are endless. Provided it comes from your heart, God will bless all the effort you put forward. Not only does it get you out of your head but it gives you a sense of purpose in life.

23

I've always received an extra measure of blessings in return for reaching out to others. Once again, only if it comes from the heart as God has already heard the best ideas from our mouths. I started writing and receiving letters from Ruth Ann Veal. She's the young lady I counseled in the early 1990's who is now serving a life sentence without the possibility of parole. It had been well over eight years since I had any correspondence with her. God blessed this from the beginning and it led to many letters, phone calls and monthly visits. Ruth Ann is now an important part of my life. Jackie, Dani and I consider her family. We pray everyday that she will be released and will come to live with us. What have I gotten out of this long distance relationship? For one thing, it's another solid reason I have not to sell out and return to my addiction.

When I became a little more sure footed in my recovery I received a call from Charlie. Charlie and I go way back to when I was 20 years old and managed a Casey's store in Pocahontas. He and his wife of many years still resided in the 'Princess City.' Charlie and Lisa were now in their lower fifties and I knew

Charlie's health had been failing for sometime but I wasn't aware of the severity. A car accident years before had left him uneasy on his feet and prone to seizures. His phone call held only one request. He wanted to go fishing. I told Charlie we would have to do just that and finally a date was set. As I arrived at Charlie's house I realized this wasn't going to be an easy task. I was greeted not only by Charlie and Lisa but by his caretaker who came in daily to bathe him and see to his needs as Lisa worked full time at the hospital.

"You ready Mike? I bet they're biting today," Charlie said smiling, sitting in his wheelchair. At his side lay two fishing poles, a large tackle box and lunch container. As I glanced into the kitchen I quickly spotted a countertop that looked like a well-stocked pharmacy shelf. Charlie was in a lot of pain and even had a Morphine pump surgically implanted inside of him. After I recovered from my 'out of body experience' seeing all those pain meds I asked if he was ready to go. That was when Lisa took me outside and explained that we would need to take the van. That vehicle was equipped with a hydraulic pulley system to lift and move Charlie's wheelchair, but getting him out of the wheelchair was a task all of its own. Charlie's legs were useless and as Lisa counted to three we lifted him from the wheelchair to a car seat that extended outside the van. Charlie was no small man, which made this quite a job. I was already thinking about when we got to the lake and it was just the two of us. Operating the lift in the rear of the van had me baffled. Saying a silent prayer and remembering the old Hollies tune, "He ain't heavy, he's my brother," we put the fishing gear in the van.

As we drove the 30 miles north to a favorite lake I confided to Charlie about the severity of my addiction. He knew I had a problem with drugs and alcohol but he didn't know the ugly details. About this time I noticed he wasn't wearing his seatbelt. That's when he explained that he's legally exempt from wearing one because of the Morphine pump. In case of an accident the seatbelt could cause the pump to discharge all the Morphine at once and that would be fatal.

"Oh," I said jokingly, "you're like a giant narcotic drink box and all I need is a straw to poke into your stomach and I'm all set." We both had a laugh while deep down I was having cravings again, maybe due to the stress of taking care of my dear friend.

We arrived at the lake on a beautiful sunny morning but were limited to fishing off the boat launch because of him being in the wheelchair. He waited patiently while I tried to retrieve the chair with a remote control. I went over and over Lisa's instructions, and saying another prayer I lowered the wheelchair to the ground with the pulley system. It actually went very well as I guided it around the van. Now I just had to get Charlie from his van seat into the wheelchair. I carefully pulled his feet and legs out and with his arm strength it was a success. Now it was time to fish as we maneuvered his electric buggy out on the boat dock. If I was alone this was the last place I would have cast my line. We didn't have that luxury I realized as I put a minnow on Charlie's hook. God blessed us richly that day as not one boat used the boat ramp. This doubting fisherman was proven wrong as Charlie reeled in a Crappie, Walleye and a Perch. Other fishermen around us were having little or no luck at all. Maybe we were just in the right place at the right time. I might have thought of this successful trip as merely luck if not for our next fishing adventure.

A month or so later my new fishing buddy called. "Hey Mike, I heard the Walleyes are biting at Storm Lake." Reluctantly I agreed as I knew we would have to fish off of a boat dock again. This is a trophy Walleye lake and you just don't catch them off of the dock. Besides it was a weekend and most likely the boats would be in and out all day. So off to Storm Lake we went as Charlie had high hopes. I, on the other hand, wasn't that confident. I knew the Walleyes were biting because of the solo trips I had recently made. I even caught an eight pounder just weeks before but my hot spots were of no use to us as these places were unfishable for my friend in his wheelchair. I must admit, as we got settled to fish off the boat dock I had a selfish moment, wanting to be across the lake where I knew they were biting. I said to myself, 'Mike, this isn't about you so calm down and enjoy the day with your friend.' It's so hard for me to fish like a normal person and truly enjoy some companionship. I got out of my head after reminding myself why we were there.

Charlie soon reeled in a nice Catfish, not a Walleye, but he was excited. What happened next I'll never forget as long as I live. An hour into our fishing trip the Walleye suddenly started biting. Believe me when I tell you this isn't a species of fish that you catch off a dock! Charlie's favorite fish came to take whatever offering he put out there. During all this I hooked and lost a heavy fish while casting with a twister. This was totally nuts as once again there were no fish being caught around us. A boat came in from a day's fishing with no fish and there we sat on the boat ramp catching Walleyes!

Then Charlie wanted to try some special lure that he ordered off the T.V. late one night. He was watching an infomercial and what they were selling would have made any Iowa fisherman an easy target. "Order now and catch Walleyes!" That's just what Charlie did. He asked me to tie one on for him, interrupting my frantic casting for the twin to the one I just lost. As I laid down my rod I thought, 'Why would you want to change baits again? After all, you're catching Walleyes!' He told me the sales pitch he heard as I tied on the painted spoon. 'Good luck with that,' I thought. He asked me if I wanted to try one, as his Walleye killer kit came in many different colors and sizes. I told him I'd rather stay with my trusty black twister. Charlie made his first cast with his infomercial piece of painted metal. As I noticed him retrieving the lure much too fast for a Walleye he shouted that he had one.

"Yeah right," I said, "you probably just snagged a Carp!"

"Carp your ass!" Charlie shouted as he fought this fish, finally handing me the pole to land it. I walked the fish down the dock to the boat ramp and finally saw it. It was a Walleye, a big Walleye! Just then the fish came off, and I apologized to Charlie for losing his fish. When he asked me what it was I humbly told him it was a Walleye, a nice one. Even more humbly I asked if I could tie on one of those magic spoons. We left for home that day with two limits of nice Walleyes and stories of the big ones that got away. Tired and exhausted Charlie fell asleep in his easy chair after telling Lisa all about our successful trip. I was pretty much spent myself as I cleaned Walleyes so Charlie and Lisa could enjoy a fish fry sometime. There I stood, tired and hungry, thinking about my drive home. As I filleted the fish I found myself reading the labels on the ten or so pill bottles. I was quickly reminded of my constant cravings. My disease told me that I could help myself. Who would know? The opportunity to score on some potent painkillers was right in front of me.

I thought to myself that God would know and I would know. What a way to spoil this miracle day that I was blessed to be a part of. Besides, these were Charlie's and he and Lisa obviously

trusted me or these pills would have been hidden. God slapped
me in the face as Lisa thanked me for taking Charlie fishing. I
regained my senses and had a nice drive back to Carroll.

During my trip home I laughed at myself when I thought
about Charlie taking his afternoon medicine at the lake. As I got
him water out of the cooler all I heard was, 'Oh crap!' He
pointed at a capsule floating in the lake that he dropped. 'You
don't even want to know what that was,' he said. I took one
look at the pill tossing around in the waves and said, "Is that an
Oxycontin?" As Charlie replied, "Good guess," I let him know
that was too much information for me, unless he wanted to see
me performing a twisted version of bobbing for apples. We both
had a good laugh over that one. Charlie and I did manage to
make one more trip in October. I could tell my friend had lost
some ground since our last trip. It seemed like his doctor had
him well medicated as he dozed in and out most of the day.

Unbeknownst to us this would be our last fishing trip
together. My life long friend and true fishing buddy passed
away that January. I miss you Charlie and thanks so much for
all the memories. God even blessed us on our last outing
together. We only fished a short time as Charlie was so physically weak. It was a beautiful Indian summer day and we
caught fish off the dock again. I have a treasured memory
from that day. It's half a fishing rod and it hangs proudly with
my others. You see, I had another big Walleye bite and this
one didn't get away. My pole broke in half as I lifted it out of
the water onto the dock. Thank you Lord for putting Charlie
back in my life after all those years. I was blessed to not only
be at his hospital bedside but was honored to have the family
request me as a pallbearer at the funeral. As Jackie and I
passed a Casey's store on our way home I looked at her and

told her that I could really use a drink. Jackie agreed but said we weren't going too.

We didn't and I held on in recovery by attending meetings and continuing to grow spiritually. I took on another service project as Jackie, Dani and I became a 'Fun Family' at nearby Quakerdale, the same boys and girl's home, just in a different town, that I had spent seven months at some 35 years earlier. I have had the privilege of mentoring two young men there who were about the same age I was when I was a resident there. I was asked to speak at Quakerdale to these special kids who got off to a rough start in their lives. They even honored me by asking that I be a guest speaker at their annual fundraiser. I was receiving the fruits of my labors in serving God and others; more important though was that I stayed clean and sober for another 24 hours. Even then the 'creep from the deep' came calling. The cravings would seemingly come out of nowhere. When I turned on the radio and heard Taco John's advertising their 'six pack and a pound' I wasn't thinking about food!

24

I pretty much just listen to positive music while in recovery. I'll tell you why I do this. Television news is depressing; questionable politicians, abortion, priests molesting children and man's inhumanity toward man. It's more than enough to make this addict want to numb his feelings. They say, "Pain is inevitable, but suffering is optional." Today I choose not to suffer so much. For a while televised sports were somewhat safe for me to watch until the commercials did me in. Radio and T.V. ads that most people find annoying or amusing can set back my recovery. Beer and liquor ads are triggers; sometimes I just change the channel. To me the Iowa lottery ads are like fingernails on a chalkboard. To promote gambling, the ads are upbeat and positive, on the other hand, the 1-800-BETS-OFF commercials are depressing and negative. The casino commercials are the same, happy and exciting, unless you cross that line and can't go back. I may be a struggling addict with a gambling problem but I don't believe you can have it both ways!

Pharmaceutical ads get to me the most. 'Is your hair falling out?' 'Are you making too many trips to the bathroom?' 'Are your kids too fat?' 'Then you must try our super prostate formula!' '… the purple pill!' or '… fat whacker!' Pharmacy spots tell me that you can now get flavored drugs so your kids won't complain about the taste. That particular ad boasted 23 different flavors. Of course my thought at the time was, 'I wonder if bubblegum flavored Morphine is as good as it sounds?' My least favorite commercial featured a pill playground to promote a nationwide pharmacy. What exactly is a pill playground anyway? My sick brain came up with these attractions: the capsule downhill slide, monkey barbiturates, pill hill, merry-go-round tranquilizers, the ever popular painkiller roller coaster, mood swings and of course the assorted party animals. Like I said earlier, adding some humor to these ads helps me cope and keeps me from making a trip to the pill playground.

I fell victim to emotional turmoil many times at my work-place. I remember one day I encountered a major attack. I had a problem swallowing that bitter pill called acceptance. You know the one that reminds us that we are powerless over people, places, things and situations. The fact that we can have no peace of mind until we can accept life on life's terms. How soon we forget that when the lower power comes calling. All it took to send me into a relapse on this day was a fellow employee lacking simple common sense. I'm sure my emotional circuits were already on overload as this same situation on a different day might have been just another minor upset. I gave some excuse to my supervisor as to why I had to leave. I called the pharmacy and was granted a painkiller refill but God was mak-ing it harder and harder. With those 'emotional turmoil remov-ers' waiting at the pharmacy I just needed to stop home for a blank check. I didn't carry cash or checks with me for this very reason. As I arrived home I ran into a snag as Jackie was there with one of our granddaughters. Still upset I ran to the convenience store for a couple of quick beers to take the edge off. I swear those pills were driving me crazy, knowing they were just sitting at the pharmacy in that white bag. I finished the beer and went home with one of my wildest lies ever.

I sunk to a new low, telling Jackie I needed a check blank to make a donation at work for an employee's children who were extremely ill. Jackie didn't question me as I did things like this in recovery. I sold out and entered the world of lies that quick and what was my excuse? Just another employee with more air in her head than common sense. In reality who was I to judge anyone, unless I was to be judged for my actions. To live and let live eluded me that day.

I haven't used our computer in years. It's been so long that I wouldn't even have a clue how to operate one today. This is a blessing all on its own. I understand you can now get mood altering pills over the internet. That would be nothing short of eventual suicide for this addict. I also thank God that he removed the weekly lotto numbers from my memory that I chose when Powerball started. It's like bondage, being shackled and chained to those precious numbers. What if you don't play but your numbers come up? I don't need that pressure in my life interfering with any spiritual progress I might have made. Worse of all, what if I did win the jackpot, I truly believe that it would be a signature on my death certificate.

I made two more serious relapse attempts before I wanted God's promises more than the numbness my disease promises and that's the secret for me anyway. Surrender to this higher power, have faith in His will for your life and, of course, H.O.P.E., Hold On Pray Everyday. My last two pill searches were futile and pathetic as I choose not to feel instead of hitting my knees and humbly asking for God's help. The first slip up was planned, after one of those draining weeks at work. I worked a half a day on Friday and came home with a serious case of poor-me's. I went to our phone book, which was like poison in this state of mind. I turned to the physician yellow pages and started to feel comforted. That comfort soon turned to pain as it does when the minister side of my brain battles with my AK-47 side. I wanted the painkillers a little more than I wanted God's help. At that point a physician's ad stood out and devoured me as I had already made my choice.

It was perfect, too perfect. An out of town doctor's office that was open on Saturday morning in a town with a lake I had never been to. Who knows, maybe when I wake up in the morning this craving will have passed. I didn't make an appointment so I wouldn't be locked in. I can honestly say this though, I just bet I didn't pray that night when I went to bed which means I wanted to use a little more than I wanted God's help. My disease tells me not to pray because God, who has all the power, may interfere with my plans. You see, in my nightly prayers I always thank God for my sobriety that day and ask that if it be his will, that he keep me clean and sober tomorrow. This is a hell of a spot to be in and is mental torture I've inflicted on myself many times.

My faith took a backseat once again and fear was behind the wheel. I awoke early that Saturday and was hell bent on getting some painkillers. After all, I'm justified; I am in pain, lots of pain. The problem is narcotic painkillers aren't designed for emotional and spiritual pain. God helped me so many times when I laid down my arms of rebellion and ran into his arms of refuge, but self-will running rampant is the opposite of surrender. Telling Jackie I was going fishing I put two poles in my car.

After all, the doctors office didn't open until 8:00 and I left at 5:00, leaving plenty of time to check out the lake. Oh, I checked out the lake alright, I drove around it but fishing wasn't my drug of choice that day. So off to the clinic I went and sat in the parking lot for close to an hour. Finally a nurse showed up and I told her I needed to see the doctor.

I swear she looked right through me as she explained that the doctor wouldn't be in that day, there had been a death in his family and he would be gone for a few days. I've never been able to take no for an answer when I'm in this state of despair. I drove to the nearest convenience store and frantically flipped through their phone book. I spotted a clinic just seven miles up the road and I was off. This was another one clinic town and it was closed. By now I was an hour and a half from home and feeling defeated. Then it hit me like a bolt of lightning, this bogus fishing trip wasn't God's will for me. I humbly drove home, telling Jackie that the fish weren't biting. I resumed my recovery and ever so gradually accepted God's purpose. Trying so hard to keep clean and sober.

Facing reality, whether it be the day to day failure and successes, holidays, changing of seasons, birthdays, anniversaries, loss of loved ones or a family crisis was quite tough when the voice of addiction came calling. My last relapse of any significance came when Jackie suddenly got very sick. While working at K-Mart she had a reoccurring bout with kidney stones. Nobody thought anything of it as she had had them many times before. This time it turned out to be a potentially fatal infection. Sasha, Dani and I rushed to the hospital as Jackie was prepared for emergency surgery. When I arrived at the hospital I noticed the name of a back pain doctor I'd heard about painted on the glass to his office. As I sat with Jackie, trying to comfort her, I was filled with anxiety and panic. Sasha and Dani went to grab a quick lunch in the hospital cafeteria and asked if I wanted to join them. I declined, saying I had to run home for a moment and then return to their mom.

Almost in a daze I went down the elevator and out the door. I was physically shaken and just wanted that chemical relief. As I entered the doctor's office the nurse took one look at me and just assumed it was back pain. She stated that the doctor was at lunch but as soon as he returned she would get me in. As I sat there waiting I thought about what would happen if Sasha and Dani walked by and saw me there. How ugly would that look? Mom was awaiting surgery and Dad is trying to escape reality again. Just then a longtime friend came in, making a delivery for the company he worked for. It was like he saw that look in my eye. He asked me what I was doing, well knowing my history with narcotic painkillers. The lies instantly returned as they always do. I told him that my back had been bothering me at work and they had sent me here for an x-ray. As he left the office my guilt was too much as I regained my senses.

I told the nurse I would just go home and lay down. She said it was obvious how much pain I was in and the doctor would be here shortly. After all, I had already filled out the paperwork, which was just more lies. She was persistent, as was my urge for some pills to get me through Jackie's ordeal. The doctor soon came in and x-rayed my back, finding nothing of course but he did give me a prescription for Vicodin. I went through 30 in two days and called back, saying they weren't working. They gave me 30 Ultram and I was all set to endure Jackie's crisis.

Monday morning came around as it always does and Jackie was doing better. I was a basket case though. The pills were gone already and I was feeling the G.S.R.'s; guilt, shame and remorse. So there I sat, exactly where I sit at this very moment thinking about the door I just opened to receive more painkillers. My heart told me to close that door right away.

So less than a week after seeing that physician and getting two painkiller prescriptions I was writing another letter. I mailed it that very morning, before I could change my mind. I felt a great sense of relief, dropping it in the mailbox, not to mention the shame of having to admit to another doctor that I had conned him. This doctor was just doing his job and the blame falls on me, not on his staff.

25

I have abstained from mood altering substances for quite some time again. That is, until the most recent sell out I just talked about in the first couple of pages of this book, and that brings me back to the present, July 2007. The last four months of sobriety have been nothing short of blissful. Still being jobless has allowed me the time and incentive to tell my story. The good Lord has blessed me with many successful fishing trips this spring. I also have the hope of returning to my favorite waters this fall. I know to my very core that alcohol or drugs would destroy this hope. I see clearly now that chasing these underwater creatures is not my only calling. As my God tells me; Go F.I.S.H., Find, Inspire, Share, Hope.

While I'm on the subject of fishing I feel compelled to share with you two 'not so memorable' trips while I struggled with recovery over the years, the first being with one of my former sons-in-law. We'll call this trip 'Mike and Ike in the Afternoon.' Sasha had mentioned several times that he was interested in going fishing with me sometime. So off the two of us went to one of my favorite farm ponds. It was the Fourth of July and quite hot that afternoon.

Since it was a holiday I was stocked up on pills and was enjoying that painkiller high. The pond was in its summer bloom with weed cover some ten feet from shore. Since I was expecting this I brought two of my belly boats, inner tubes, for us to float in beyond the weed cover and fish the open water. We each had a cloth sack that hung from our inner tube. We quickly started filling these bags with Crappie and Perch. If you're not familiar with belly boats, just picture a round inner tube. You step inside it, walking to the deeper water. Soon your feet are off of the bottom and you are sitting comfortably in the cross section in the lower part of the inner tube. We both wore shorts so our bare legs were dangling in the water. We were drifting away from each other as I noticed something in the water. There, just ahead of me, was a half of a Crappie, still bleeding. Then another and another. Each fish was just the tail half but perfectly cut just below the head.

As more and more of these mutilated fish floated around me I became a bit uneasy. Who knows, it could have been a hallucination with all of those pills and out there in the hot sun. Instinctively I reached for my bag of Crappies to pull them out of the water. As I tugged on the mesh bag I noticed that it seemed to be stuck to something. I pulled even harder and as it came up it seemed to be extremely weighed down by something. That something was a very large snapping turtle holding on for dear life as I watched fish after fish escape through the hole he tore in the bag. Just then, before panic set in, the huge turtle fell from the bag and disappeared into the water. Thank the Lord for that because anybody who knows me would tell you that some real insanity was about to take place.

Especially since I was under the influence I would have fought this snapper tooth and nail for every Crappie he stole from me. Of course I was on his turf so this prehistoric reptile would have had home field advantage. In hindsight I see how fortunate I really was as he could have easily shredded my belly boat. As for me, I probably would have ended up mangled like those Crappies did. What happened next is something only a person under the influence would do. Trying frantically to save every fish I could I folded the bag and set it in my lap inside the tube. I kicked my feet and moved a few yards away and started casting to replace those Crappies that creature stole from me. Now here's some insanity for you as it occurred to me where I set those fish. Looking down at my crotch I saw a bag of fish that were still quite alive. What if that turtle, who's already tasted the fruits of my labor, returns for more? This time the fish that Mr. Snapping Turtle craved were lying on my private parts. Jackie and I hadn't planned on having any more children but the thought of an underwater vasectomy was just too much for me to worry about.

I hollered at my son-in-law who was some distance away and we did the foot paddle thing until we finally met up. Telling of my encounter with 'Turtlezilla' we put what fish I had left in his bag. Needless to say we fished right next to each other the rest of the day. The bag he had was made of solid fabric not the mesh that mine was. Soon it was time for me to return to my car for more pills so we beached our watercraft and headed home. As Jackie and Sasha fired up the grill I told them the story, somewhat inflated by now of course.

My second 'not so memorable' trip came while in recovery, still struggling as always. Let's call this story 'Fishing With Lenny.' Lenny is a friend of mine who shares some common interests, fishing and living life one day at a time. We live about 25 miles apart and his favorite Catfish lake is about 10 miles from his house. The plan was for some overnight fishing at a lake I had never been to. After darkness set in we met at a Dairy Queen and I followed him to the lake. I didn't have a clue where we were, especially in dark, as he pulled over and parked. To my surprise a truck pulled up and Lenny explained that a friend of his would be joining us. I don't like surprises and besides, there was already another vehicle parked close by that had my attention.

The young couple inside had obviously been drinking by their tone of voice. So Lenny introduced me to his friend, assuring me that he was also in recovery and a good fishing buddy. The three of us gathered up our equipment and proceeded to where we would fish. We had just got settled with our lines in the water when we heard a noise behind us. It was the young man from the vehicle that caught my eye just a short time earlier.

"Is that a 357 Magnum you got strapped to your side?" I heard a drunken voice yell from the pitch black. Just then Lenny's friend yelled, "What's it to ya?" I'm quietly sitting there thinking, 'Oh my god, this guy brought a gun fishing!' The young stranger, obviously feeling no pain, then said, "I had mine stolen. Mind if I take a look at it?" Lenny's friend responded, "Yeah, I mind a lot!" The drunk then started making accusations toward the three of us. He said that we were buddies of some guy in prison. He threatened that he knew where we were from and what we were up to. Here all this time I thought we were three lost souls in recovery out for a peaceful nights fishing. So much for peaceful as Lenny's friend challenged this aggressive drunk in the dark.

"If you have enough guts why don't you come over here and see what kind of gun it is!" Right about here I started praying silently, sitting on my bucket in the darkness. During my prayer I couldn't help but overhear the words 'Go ahead and shoot me!' Something not good was about to happen as I prayed even harder. Just as suddenly the drunk kid backed off and grumbled, "Ah it's probably just a knife anyway." I thanked God again and again as he staggered away, especially after finding out it was a gun, a loaded gun, strapped to the side of Lenny's friend.

I've heard since that this young intruder ended up in prison for another incident. God protected the three of us that night and answered my prayer, this I know. Looking back it has all the makings of a bad recovery joke. Three recovering drug addicts, a drunk and a loaded gun. Believe me; it was anything but funny that night.

Now I'd like to share a few lighthearted stories. Over the years I've written three journals covering the torment and pitfalls of trying to live clean and sober. When I looked through them to prepare this book I could once again feel the awful pain of early recovery. On and off recovery when you really want it is even more gut wrenching. The real healing though seemed to come when I found a way to attach some humor to life's set-backs. I'd like to highlight just a few. These still make me smile. Earlier in my insanities I told of taking our cat and dogs medication. I do believe I've made amends over the years for those selfish acts.

Let's start with our 225 pound Mastiff, Rameses. Today we have an unbreakable bond. Most days when Jackie and Dani are at work it's just us two guys. He listens to my woes and dilemmas and doesn't criticize. He just stands there wagging his huge tail. My amends to him are exhibited everyday as he seems to have me on a pretty short leash. Then there's our cat, Pumpkin. Taking all of her seizure medicine and then leaving her alone was a bit more dangerous than eating a couple of Rameses's dog biscuit painkillers. She did get some sweet revenge one night as I was down on my knees cleaning out her litter box. Since we have three cats I was trying to save a little money on litter by picking out all the kitty turds. As I'm throwing them in a bag I turn around and there's Pumpkin, just staring at me. She was showing no gratitude and surely thinking, 'Are you done yet? I gotta take a crap!' I had a humble moment as I realized she still holds some resentment. That Christmas she got a second chance at payback. Jackie and Dani got her some catnip toys as presents and as she rolled around on the floor getting high I stood there quite envious. We've been okay with each other ever since.

When I'm in recovery I find I'm much more helpful around the house, compared to drinking and popping pills, when I'm just another family burden. Doing some of these household chores though, can trigger my insanity. Let's start with dishes. Did you know you have to wash them before you put them in the dishwasher? What's up with that? Why not just dry them then and put the suckers in the cupboard? Doing laundry really boggles my mind. I've noticed that most every article of clothing came out of our dryer inside out. Being the problem solver that I am, I had an idea. I put everything in the dryer inside out. I thought to myself that no machine is going to outfox this addict. Guess what? They still came out inside out! Go figure. Then there's the washing machine and all its settings. I always wondered at meetings when the topic of normal people was going to come up. I thought to myself, what exactly is normal? Now I know from doing laundry it's nothing more than a setting on a washing machine! What articles of clothing you can and can't put together is another dilemma. Dani went through a phase of buying clothes with little bits of glitter all over them. I washed them with my shirts and went to a prison recovery meeting that night. Jackie had a good laugh that night when I came home and stood under the light. I had tiny sparkles all over my face! I can only imagine what the inmates thought as I sat there sharing my experience, strength and hope. 'Who's this guy looking like Tinkerbell?' Needless to say, Dani's clothes with sparkles don't get washed with my shirts anymore!

26

I have come to realize that my head has invisible antenna's attacked to it. I'm constantly receiving thoughts, some good, some bad and some quite insane. My chiropractor, also in recovery, explained this to me. He told me to stop beating myself up over thoughts I couldn't control. I now thank God for the good thoughts and have a thing I do when the crazy ones enter. I tug on my right ear lobe to thank God for the good thoughts. When the negative ones enter I tug on my left earlobe, this flushes them down the toilet. On bad days I even picture them swirling and disappearing. Of course, it's up to me not to grab my mental plunger and pull them right back up. Some doctors call this mind racing and of course they have plenty of medications that can help. No thanks, with God's help my system is working.

It's important to think the thought, don't repress it. Let it come into reality. Then, if it's a good thought cherish it, if it's a bad thought flush it. This chiropractor shared a wise quote with me one day as he tried to ease my pain without the crutch of narcotics. I'll never forget that he suggested I do the following:

1. Take no credit.
2. Accept no praise.
3. Place no blame.
4. Pass no judgment.
5. Let the healing field in.

Thanks to this gentleman I learned pain control without feeding my addiction. He did tell me one day that it would to okay to take an occasional baby aspirin. I must admit in my state of constant cravings I laughed all the way home. A baby aspirin? This man of wisdom suddenly wasn't so wise, or was he?

Humility for me is indispensable, as false pride most certainly cometh before the fall. While I was being detoxed in Omaha a man from the outside shared his hope in recovery. After telling his story he passed out a small card to each of us. The card reads as follows: 'Prayer for Humility: Lord, I am far too much influenced by what people think of me. This means that I am always pretending to be either richer or smarter or nicer than I really am. Please prevent me from trying to attract attention. Don't let me gloat over praise on the one hand or be discouraged by criticism on the other. Nor let me waste time weaving imaginary situations in which the most heroic, charming or witty person present is myself. Show me how to be humble of heart like you. Amen.'

For me to stay clean and sober there are certain rock solid must do's. I've mentioned the importance of God, meetings and service. The other words of recovery for me are surrender, humility, acceptance, gratitude, perseverance and hope. I witnessed so many souls finishing treatment and going back into society with that treatment high. If the tools of recovery aren't sharpened each and everyday they go dull in a hurry. One mistake I see with those leaving treatment is that 'their brain gets smart but their head stays dumb.' The creep from the deep is quick to devour those who let their spiritual tools go dull. Plain and simple early recovery sucks, but we must persevere. You may think it doesn't get any better but it does. Time and patience are key elements to my success.

In my own personal experience with the early stage of recovery I can honestly tell you it's slow and painful. You must remember; if there's no pain there's no gain. We used to cover the pain with drugs and alcohol and didn't hold out for our miracle. Sometimes the best I could do in early recovery was to claim God's victory in my struggles one day at a time. I remember, after leaving treatment for the first time, seeing my mother in church every week. After the service mom would come close to me, look into my eyes and ask if it was getting any better. She asked this week after week. Finally one week I held up my thumb and index finger, showing a tiny gap between them.

"Mom," I said, "it gets about this much better every week. Sometimes though, it takes two weeks to gain this little bit." My poor mother, without a clue really, just stood there, loving her son and I'm sure many prayers were said for me. The cool thing is though, that tiny gap of improvement or spiritual progress every week or two, continues to widen, provided I'm working my program of recovery. In the months that followed the gap became large enough that I felt comfortable in my own skin. That word, Gap, which I've since seen on clothing, has a special significance. Gratitude, Acceptance, Patience. This reminder was shared with me by a very special young lady. Sadly, a short time later, while driving under the influence, her life changed forever. The life of an innocent person was taken in a fatal car accident.

Alcohol and drugs don't only take the life of the abuser but it all too often takes the lives of others. My friend, a wife and mother, now spends her days behind prison walls. Oh the anguish of doing something in an instant that changes the lives of so many forever.

My plea to all of you who are abusing prescription medications, street drugs or alcohol is to stop before it's too late. There's no separating the three. I believe that a drug is a drug is a drug whether it comes from a pharmacy, a back alley or a store shelf. All three are equal opportunity destroyers. It's truly Russian Roulette. As Clint Eastwood once said in a movie, 'Do ya feel lucky punk? Well do ya?' It's not too late for you if you're reading this. I've heard it said that, 'To get to a place we've never been we must follow a path we've never taken.' For me that path begins and ends with God the Father, God the Son and God the Holy Spirit. Too large of a chunk of my life was spent in a tug of war with God until one day I came to realize that the only one tugging was me. On the other end was God, the rope was lying at his feet. His loving hand not pulling against me, but extended toward me, just waiting for me to surrender and lay down the rope. "Come to me, all you who are weary and burdened, and I will give you rest." Matthew 11:28.

27

Right here I need to mention some very special people who lost their lives to this disease called addiction and alcoholism. Believe me, these are just a few of the countless lives that are lost everyday where alcohol or drugs contributed. I've mentioned Diane and Tim earlier whose lives were cut short by the grip of alcoholism and addiction. Another young man and woman were from Pocahontas. Rachel drank herself to death over the years after she and loved ones suffered through her inability to give up the drink and live a sober life.

Chet was my next door neighbor for a short time. A few months before his death he sat on his front porch drinking. He called out to me, asking if I wanted a beer. He continued as Jackie and I, barely 20 years old at the time, tried to ignore him. As we turned out the lights to go to bed Chet drank alone. That Memorial Day, after some heavy drinking and paying his respects to friends lost in Vietnam, he returned home. Walking by his child and his child's mother he went upstairs. She held their son as the gun went off above them. Chet had just taken his life. I have suffered through many emotions over this event that happened nearly 35 years ago. My missed opportunity to visit with him that night still bothers me.

Alice struggled with pills and alcohol. I, along with others, listened to her dilemmas and woes many times. She faded in and out of sobriety, feeling more and more guilty each time she gave into her disease. Alice lived close by where we met many Sunday mornings. Another friend in recovery drove by Alice's house one morning on his way to the meeting. His concern led to the discovery that Alice had taken her own life with the help of her loosing battle with substance abuse and depression. Alice lost her hope in a painful moment. That must be the feeling that tortures us the most, the feeling of hopelessness.

Amy, a young lady, only twenty-nine years old, left treatment and over dosed on meth a day or two later. Besides her grieving family, Amy left behind a son. Her picture, shown with her obituary, is a strong statement to the powerful nature of addiction. This photo of Amy, smiling and vibrant, wearing a Tommy Girl shirt, would bring tears to even the most coldhearted drug dealer.

Finally, my friend George, who I think of every time I hear the whistle of a passing train. The entry in my journal on June 13, 2006 reads like this: 'Today I feel sad, emotionally shot! I lost a friend today. George passed away this morning, this was a tough loss! Oh, those missed opportunities; they always seem to haunt me! Often times because we feel that we can do little to help someone, we make the mistake of doing nothing.' The front page of our local newspaper that afternoon was controversial to say the least. In a full color photograph, there lay George next to the train tracks. His lifeless body was on exhibit next to the train that killed him. This sensationalism showed by our hometown newspaper prompted me to cancel our subscription.

I wrote an editorial to this paper and it appeared along with many others. Family and friends of George suffered needlessly by the printing of the photo and harsh words attacking his character.

I'd known George for some time prior to his death and witnessed his struggled with alcohol. George's battle between hope and hopelessness must have been hell on earth. I knew him as a spiritual, God fearing and caring man. I was blessed on many occasions to listen to the wisdom he possessed. For those who didn't really know George, this is what they read in our paper:

'Man had been drinking before stepping in front of train. The Carroll man who killed himself by stepping into the path of a freight train Tuesday morning took one last drink of beer and tossed the can aside before being struck. Police identified the man today as George, age 60. The incident occurred shortly before 10:30 A.M. on Tuesday on the Union Pacific tracks. George was thrown clear of the train and died instantly. The police chief and authorities are convinced he committed suicide. Officers searched George's residence and spoke with acquaintances and relatives. He left a note at his trailer, although it wasn't worded as a suicide note. The police chief declined to disclose the contents of the letter. 'Everything we're seeing now leads us to believe this was a suicide,' the chief said. When asked to elaborate the chief said, 'The actions immediately prior to the incident that witnesses described to us, he knew full well the train was coming, he had ample time to get out of the way, it was broad daylight, sunny and clear, 70 degrees.' Witnesses told police that George stepped into the path of the eastbound freight train, "took a drink from the can he was holding and then tossed it aside" then was hit by the lead locomotive. The body came to rest on the north side of the rails. Police removed at least two 16 ounce cans of Ice House beer from the scene. Six counts of public intoxication dating back to 1997 are among the 18 convictions on George's criminal record.'

This article was a one sided view of George and I believe exploited his spectacular death in the interest of selling newspapers. I so miss seeing him at meetings and will never forget the impact he made in my own recovery. May God comfort and bless his family and friends.

28

In closing I realize I sit here on borrowed time and am so very grateful to God for my family. At this moment my daughter Dani, finding many things out about her dad for the first time, is just behind me typing the first seventy-one pages of my scribbles. As I'm here near the end of the book and really trying to wrap this up, Jackie, bless her heart, tells me there's probably another book I could write on just the stuff I forgot. While Dani is typing, Jackie's napping after working another Saturday to pay the bills while I write. The two of them even went to the library yesterday to check out books on how to help me get published.

Sasha and my two granddaughters no longer live next door to us. Since I started this book in March Sasha got pregnant and God is blessing us with a grandson Zane. I sure miss the two little girls dropping in unexpectedly. As for my oldest daughter, another Father's Day came and went with out a call or a card. I love you Janna and hope God grants you the same peace I long for.

Just in the last four months Jackie, Sasha and Dani have turned down prescriptions for narcotics. Eighteen year old Dani still suffers from a nasty badminton accident at school last Halloween. Since having three teeth knocked out from being hit by the racket she has had many dentist appointments and surgeries on her mouth. This special young lady turned down two prescriptions for Hydrocodone, instead taking an over the counter painkiller called Ibuprofen. Dani also suffers from migraines and turned down Stadol at the emergency room instead receiving Toradol, a mild pain reliever. Jackie told me this, not Dani, how special is that?

Sasha, like her dad, suffers from frequent migraines. Her doctor handed her prescriptions for Stadol and Tylox. She was told that because of her pregnancy this was all she could safely have. Sasha left the prescriptions at the counter and returned home, taking only Tylenol. She came over to the house and we visited until her headache eased a little bit. Sasha couldn't believe what they offered her and we talked about how narcotic painkillers have their place. Sasha and Dani are just afraid to take that stuff after seeing it bring their dad to his knees.

Then there's my wife Jackie, always thinking of me despite her physical pain. She recently had a terrible cough keeping her up at night and forcing her to miss work. The doctor tried to give her cough syrup with Codeine but she declined. Jackie has done this countless times when offered a prescription for a mood altering substance. I know in the heat and humidity of an Iowa summer she would enjoy a cold beer. I also know how much Jackie liked an occasional margarita but rarely does. She allows no alcohol in our home, period. How could I break the trust of my support system at home? How could I ever relapse and throw their hopes and unconditional love out the window?

Actually, it's quite easy when you're an alcoholic and an addict. It's cunning, baffling and powerful and oh so patient.

This is why I must do it each and every day because if I don't believe I deserve a life of sobriety my disease will convince me that I don't deserve my loved ones either. This disease is used constantly by the ever-tempting lower power that is out there waiting to devour us. This creep from the deep hates our God, meetings and serving others. Just recently as I struggled for victory over the month of May the lower power tempted me again. It was late May as we sat in a hot school auditorium, during Dani's graduation. Then suddenly Jackie's dad turned to a complete stranger and said, "I bet you wouldn't turn down a cold beer if I offered you one."

It was so hot in there and we had to sit on the hard bleachers for a couple of hours. I know Jackie squirmed in her seat when she heard that statement. Her dad is 90 years old and doesn't understand addiction. God has blessed us so often through his generosity. I need to stay in an attitude of gratitude. Maybe it was the stress of Dani's big day or the heat but I started unraveling on graduation Sunday.

Sasha and I went fishing for a couple of hours afterward. On the way to the lake I confessed to her about my craving for an ice cold brew. She nodded and agreed that it sounded good on such a hot and humid afternoon. I chuckled as I realized that, in fact, I didn't want just one, but several. That's the difference between Jackie's dad and me. He has his one mixed drink every day at 4:00 P.M. and doesn't refill the glass until the next day. Just the thought of that kind of moderation drives me crazy. The normal drinker may never understand the alcoholic. Meetings are a God send as I am surrounded by loving souls that do understand. I have an empty shot glass on my desk with a rather large bullet in it. The bullet serves as a reminder that if I fill that shot glass with alcohol I just as well spend the shell first and spare myself and my family the misery.

On May 27, 2007 Jackie and I were blessed to celebrate not only our 35th anniversary but Dani's 18th birthday. I found it interesting that 35 plus 18 equals my current age, 53. By the grace of God I was alive and sober on such an occasion. The days following Dani's high school graduation and party at our house were stressful. This, combined with the poor-me's on Father's Day, set me up for emotional turmoil. As I sat where I am at this very moment the cravings hit hard.

My head wanted a break from reality as I pulled the phone book from the drawer. My Bible or the big book would have been a better choice. In moments like this I don't know exactly what happens but it is a power second only to God himself! Sure enough, I quickly found some candidates for painkillers. As I sat there drooling over the possibility of not feeling anything for that day, God intervened. My self-centered thinking left me as I re-entered my heart. I tore out the entire physician section of our phone book and threw the pages in the trashcan. It was up to me not to return to it and retrieve the temptation now covered with coffee grounds. By the grace of God I didn't and all the praise, credit and glory go to Him alone. "Even to your old age and gray hair I am He, I am He who will sustain you. I have made you and I will carry you; I will sustain you and I will rescue you." Isaiah 46:4.

We often run to the false gods of drugs and alcohol looking for rescue from life's pressures but it never lasts and ultimately destroys us. I remember my one and only fishing trip to Canada on Labor Day weekend 1989. A 30 some hour road trip found Jackie and me in a boat with two friends for just a couple days fishing, then back to work on Tuesday. As the four of us ventured out in the middle of nowhere, searching for Northern Pike, a storm was brewing. This was a small boat, to say the least, and quite outdated. Very suddenly we were in the middle of the storm. We were too far from shore so we tried to ride it out as the waves crashed against us. I can assure you I wasn't the only one praying as the storm worsened. I'm sure, like me, Jackie was thinking of our daughters back home, especially four month old Dani. I honestly don't think I've ever been that scared. Just as quickly as it started the winds died down and I shivered from the cold thanking God again and again.

I might suggest that if you ever make a fishing trip to Canada, leave the beer behind. A rain suit would be a much wiser purchase. I was literally soaked to my underwear. It was very late afternoon and getting cold when the most incredible thing happened that I've ever witnessed as a fisherman. Up to that point we had only been catching Pike in the two to four pound range. After the rain subsided the giant Pike went on a feeding frenzy. We caught and lost many Pike in the 12 to 25 pound class. I was blessed to land, with Jackie's assistance, a 27 pound trophy Pike. This monster, almost four feet long, broke our net in three pieces and now proudly hangs on our wall. Upon returning home I wrote my brother a 10 page letter telling of this miraculous fishing trip. I remember my last line of the letter reading like this, "The calm boat ride back to camp, loaded down with fish, was a high no drug could ever equal."

Of course, as you well know by now, I would challenge that statement a couple of years later. I don't know what plans God has for the other two fisherman who survived the storm that day. It's crystal clear to Jackie and me though. I believe for the same reason He has spared my life many times since. You see, just a month later I quit my job as a route salesman for Coors.

This is when I went to work as a youth counselor for Forest Ridge. Jackie and I met Ruth Ann Veal there. Jackie tells me that my life's purpose is in writing this memoir. Two things are certain, God has a vision for my life and Jackie is rarely wrong. Just the other night as she was going to bed, knowing I was distressed, she did it again.

As we kissed goodnight she said she loved me and told me to stay the course. As I was leaving the room she told me she was proud of me. I most certainly know why God kept her alive that day in Canada. Jackie is a wife, mother, grandmother, sister and daughter beyond compare. I love her more everyday. As the song says, she is truly 'the wind beneath my wings' or 'an angel walking too close to the ground.' Thank you again for your tireless support and praise. Jackie has always believed in me and picked me up as Mike the boxer often hit the canvass. 'Fall down seven times but get up eight' she reminds me. It was Jackie's extra push that got me to sit here and share my life story with you.

Jackie and Dani have each encouraged me. Those two read books constantly, unlike me who can't sit still that long. They were not too greatly surprised when I recently confided in them a little secret. The irony of me writing a book is that I've never read one cover to cover. When I sit down to re-read this manuscript it will be my first full book. Many may consider this foolish but God's foolishness is greater than human wisdom. I'll never forget a statement made by a recovering alcoholic. He stated that his 'most vivid memories were of things that never actually happened.' I assure you that's not the case with me. I well remember these events though I wish many never happened.

If not for the grace of God I would still be seeking the substance that destroys. Today I seek faith, the substance of what I hope for. In recent days I've had a chance, a reminder, to be thankful for the 24 hour reprieve from drugs and alcohol. You remember Pumpkin, the cat with nine lives. Well, now she has severe asthma. It's been my morning responsibility to mix her two medicines and conceal them in a plate of fresh tuna. So, as I'm powdering up her pills, with a razor blade no less, I'm filled with gratitude, but for the grace of God I would be starting my day like this, powdering up my pills to just get through the morning.

29

Returning home a couple weeks ago from a days fishing I received yet another reminder on the power of addiction. I hadn't been home long when I discovered some body invaders. I was covered with wood ticks. These creatures are cunning, baffling and powerful in their own right. As I picked them off one by one I thought to myself how wood ticks are like addiction. They start out small and look so innocent, just like the pills did in the beginning. Then they attach to you and dig in, slowly sucking your blood they grow in size. If they're not discovered early and removed they take over, eventually sucking the very life out of you.

There are consequences for our actions, even that most recent slip back in March. As I'm looking at the emergency room bill at this very moment I realize that an hour of pain relief cost my family $1,127.84, compare that to the cost of staying clean and sober, priceless. The 'creep from the deep' uses his tools of guilt, shame and remorse for that most recent sell out. I'm struck by the saying, "The next time the devil reminds you of your past, just remind him of his future."

The lower power may be able to take man away from God but can never take God away from man. Victory is ours when we surrender and claim it. "The word of the cross is folly to those who are perishing, but to us who are being saved it is the power of God." 1 Corinthians 1:18. One last warning about early recovery, that's brushing your teeth. The thoughts that enter your head during this simple task can make or break your day. Upon awaking, the good, the bad and the ugly thoughts come calling. For me it's quite often while I'm brushing my teeth. They usually enter without invitation, trying to crash your party or that recovery high you're on. My proven method is to embrace the good thoughts and flush the bad and ugly ones with thoughts of God. "We are afflicted in every way, but not crushed; perplexed, but not driven to despair." 2 Corinthians 4:8.

So how many days of clean time do I have? I've learned in my own personal experience not to count the days. I must claim victory in this 24 hours only by the grace of God. When I start boasting of lengthy sobriety I'm just setting myself up for a relapse. Maybe it's because I believe I don't deserve the success and all the rewards that go with doing the right thing. I will take a chance and honestly tell you that I haven't sought out any pills, alcohol or injections since that painful day in early March. Maybe, just painfully maybe, by writing this and exposing my personal battle with the disease of addiction I will receive another 24 hours. Just for today. Not Mike's will but thy will be done.

July 14, 2007

"For freedom Christ has set us free; stand firm therefore, and do not submit again to a yoke of slavery..." Galatians 5:1.

Not the end, just a new beginning.

www.ingramcontent.com/pod-product-compliance
Lightning Source LLC
Chambersburg PA
CBHW030445290526
45786CB00001B/454